Discover your subtle self

Other publications in the Mind Bathing series, based on the principles taught by Gururaj Ananda (1932–1988):

Answers to Your Life – a data CD for quick referencing subject matter in Gururaj's 300 UK talks

Guarantee to Make the Law of Attraction Work – an ebook being developed into paperback

Gems of the Heart; A Message for Your Heart – extracts from Gururaj's talks and poems

Discover your subtle self

Exploit your hidden dimensions
Attract the circumstances you desire
Diminish stress, fear and discontent

By John Lamb

Edited by Georgia Rei

Based on the author's understanding of the teachings of
Gururaj Ananda (1932–1988)

Disclaimer

The contents of this publication are in small measure the author's opinion and, largely, the teaching expounded by the author's mentor, Gururaj Ananda Yogi (1932–1988) as interpreted by the author. Neither the publisher nor the author offer professional advice to the individual reader. None of the ideas, practices and suggestions in this book are intended as a substitute for medical advice, which should be sought from health care professionals, i.e. suitably qualified physicians. Neither the author nor the publisher shall be liable or responsible for any loss or damage allegedly arising from any information or suggestion in this book. All content shall be treated as opinion.

First published in the United Kingdom in 2011
by Subeam Publications
Produced by The Choir Press

ISBN 978–0–9569025–0–4

Contents

Dedicated, with unending thanks, to an incredible mentor, Gururaj Ananda, and in memory of one of his ardent followers, the late Constance Joan Gibson (Oxford, UK) who sponsored this production.

Prologue

Several decades prior to the recent world-wide curiosity in The Law Of Attraction, Gururaj Ananda Yogi (1932–1988) had issued to his followers practical, workable instructions on how to control thought so as to engender a life full of satisfaction.

You can read a review of Gururaj's life in the appendices of this book. His recorded teachings include exceedingly simple solutions for resolving why most people who attempt to use the Law Of Attraction – and other universal laws – oftentimes do not succeed. Most people don't get to a state of entire satisfaction in life, whether they are attempting to use the Law of Attraction or not. But thousands of Gururaj's students can testify to the effectiveness of his techniques which are unspeakably discerning.

It's no coincidence that the majority of Gururaj's students are living to a ripe old age, enjoying good health. And they often look young for their age, have all the love they want, material wants are fulfilled and they have peace in their lives.

Everyone has a subtle mind, which is the ordinary logic mechanism infused with as much subtle energy as possible. We use subtle energy by accessing many layers of finer energy vibrations, both inside and outside of our make up. Using the subtle mind expediently can solve our problems and our needs – and most desires too.

Users of subtle energy have convincing 'inner feelings' much of the time. They throw their minds open in a certain way and solutions to the largest of problems appear from unexpected sources.

Other advantages often occur too. For example,
- sensing what other people are about to think or do, via vibrational attunement
- sensing what is bad for health (against the majority view)
- being guided away from danger / defending oneself
- glimpsing multi-dimensional one-ness – the only actual state of being – thereby solving 'the riddle of life'
- acquiring material stuff or personal qualities (using the Law of Attraction)
- overcoming fear and reducing the effects of stress
- revitalising relationships

The benefits build and build. Using subtle energy doesn't provide an instant fix to everything. The changes that come grow with repetitive use. Some effort is required to get all the advantages on offer but the rewards are truly worth pursuing.

Introduction

Your ordinary mind relates everything to solid matter, which, according to sub-atomic investigation, we now know is not real.

Most people allow the solid state we perceive to severely limit their lives by not addressing the possibility of going beyond the limitation of sensory input.

However, subtle energy is everywhere and is available in its fullness every nanosecond in time. Using it, instead of either denying it or not bothering with it, can change your life into whatever you want it to be without any more effort than you put in previously. So, it's a matter of choice whether to accept your lot, as the saying goes – even when this includes a lot of buffeting around and not reaching your goals – or whether you turn the key to engender a life of happiness and fulfilment.

This book focuses on the state you can achieve during this lifetime where you overcome the restrictions of your conditioned mind, by utilising subtle energy.

Your individuality and your consciousness are evolving at a rate unwittingly set by you. The three-dimensional trap in which you are now caught up brings about all your problems. Once you pull free from the trap you can start flowing with your natural evolution (again). Your old 'solid-mind' thinking process will no longer be your puppeteer. You then have much more control over your evolution including your lifetime here.

To understand exactly how to achieve this position of renewed self power is as simple as reading an instruction manual. Whether or not you use the information you glean is entirely up to you.

There are three stages the book lays out.

The first stage is identifying yourself. This means basing your understanding of life in terms of what you really are, how you are evolving and how your 'stuck' mind patterning, which severely limits you, can be overcome. We explore the process of life cycles which predetermine your present existence and how you brought yourself here in the first place.

Secondly, practising what the author calls *mind bathing* is described – stilling techniques so simple and energising / stress relieving / life-solving they can only be described as delicious.

Thirdly, 'unconditioning' is highlighted. Almost everyone has an unconscious, inbuilt resistance to getting out of life what they would really like. If you employ unconditioning you can discover what your resistance is and turn your life around quickly. We look at triggers and tools that can be used to put this into effect.

All three 'prongs', above, come under the banner of *mind bathing*. To get most benefit, it's pointless using one prong without the other two. The outcome of bringing them into daily life is an adjustment in perspective allied to a calmer, more positive and balanced outlook. The old stolid thinking process gradually gets replaced by your free, unencumbered mind, which is empowered by dimensions of your being previously beyond grasp. You recognise immediately the (re) kick-starting of the subtle energy flow within you.

Most people don't change instantly because their image of life is challenged by new ideas of perception. But, once you open your mind to all possibilities, which this book helps you to do, it doesn't take long to appreciate that your multi-dimensional, ultra powerful self is existent and useable.

Your self-built barriers to ultimate happiness can be broken down and dispensed with. Your birthright is infinite self power and nothing can stand in your way, except your restricted thinking process, which can be subtly readjusted, once you get to grips with the principles herein.

1

Mind Interpretation Versus Your Reality

"Life is a continuum. It is not a number of decades during which each animal, human or plant ingests oxygen; nor even the number of millennia each planet takes to appear and disappear. You can confirm this in your own consciousness." – Author

Knowledge and Belief

What is life and what is death?

Life is generally regarded as being the experiences of your independent mechanism of flesh, organs, blood and bones from the moment you pop out of your mother's body – or from the time of conception if you prefer to think that way – until you expire. Your death is said to be the moment in which you finish your last breath; everything stops and life expires.

From what viewpoint is this description made? It is made from the viewpoint of the human mind.

Most of us have no knowledge about anything beyond this solid, three-dimensional state. But what you see within the scope of the five senses is nothing more than a minuscule reflection of *actual* existence.

The human mind relates only to what is perceived as solid matter. It is the mind that tells you one state is a living state and another state is a dead state.

Because the human mind is exceedingly limited it is not much use trying to consider life as a whole phenomenon, including states beyond the mortal frame. Asking the mind to conceptualise a multi-dimensional phenomenon just doesn't work.

The mind works on imagination and belief. Belief is a substitute for knowledge. Belief fills in the gap where knowledge is not existent. If you have knowledge you don't need belief.

You can confirm the existence of your whole Self by *experience*. And, if you have that experience, you won't need to use belief any longer.

You do not need to become a mystic to understand that *whole* life includes states of being other than an active mind in a breathing, blood-circulating mechanism. Eminent scientists have already uncovered the fact that there are many more (finer dimensional) states of existence superimposed on what we perceive with our five senses.

With this updated understanding in place, we have no further need to subject ourselves to conjecture. We can move forward from belief systems based on guesswork. We can rely on certain knowledge.

The discovery of more, finer dimensional, states will soon lead us to the automatic adjustment of much outdated religious dogma which, in recent millennia, was foisted upon us by would-be controllers and, occasionally, kind-spirited good samaritans. Much of this incomplete information was passed on in good faith but a good deal of it was the work of power freaks who wanted to control other people by means of fear (of the unknown).

I am not recommending you throw away your religion if you have one. All religions contain the seeds of truth. But when you *know* the truth of existence within yourself, you can deepen your faith and at the same time move beyond the idea of a Santa Claus type judge waiting for you in the far beyond.

By perceiving your *wholeness* you can become an honest, potent force in your own evolution. You can put suffering behind you. You can plan to streamline your excursions beyond this little life. You can master the universes, seen and unseen. You can liberate your soul.

Dimensions

To start, what do we actually know?

Everything, large or small, including every person and every cell or atom, has dimensional counterparts superimposed upon it. Scientists are now certain of this. They are calling these added dimensions 'shadow' energy or 'dark' energy. This includes all forms of energy that are known but unseen, including thought.

These subtle counterparts are imperceptible to our five senses. But we can now state with certainty that man/woman is multi-dimensional and not just three-dimensional.

We continue, for the time being, with our deep rooted *limited* perception, because we are preoccupied with what is solid – or what appears to be solid. It seems to us that solid matter is the realness of life.

Until recently, anything we thought of as existing 'in the ether' was more or less taboo. It was also considered more likely to be peripheral to, or in addition to, the physical universe which we have previously relied on to be our reality.

However, if we think from a multi-dimensional standpoint we can start to imagine the truer perspective of an infinite, multi-dimensional wholeness of which three-dimensional existence is just a compressed, limited angle of reflection.

One problem we have is how to think from a multi-dimensional viewpoint, when we largely have great difficulty in grasping what another dimension really is. Is it another sphere? If so, how can we imagine a sphere in terms of existence? How can we add one dimension to our lives or take one away?

Because the answers to these questions are difficult to comprehend, I once concocted a tale in an attempt to explain, to students of all ages, how to relate to this subject. It is an allegory that Gururaj, my mentor, urged me to publish. I will tell the tale now in the hope that it helps to clarify the issue.

Remember, all dimensions are here and now. They are not at some other place or some other time.

The Allegorical Tale of Wunspot

Wunspot, whose name is derived from 'one spot', is a little being. We, in our three dimensional preoccupation, can't see or feel him (or her) because Wunspot lives in a world consisting of one dimension only. He is so tiny that he has no width or height. We humans can't actually locate Wunspot but we are aware that a single dimension definitely exists. We are certain of this because we know one dimension is the straight line distance from one point to another.

Another word for a straight line is a radian. A radian is a straight line of no definitive length and it doesn't have to be visible. As I've said, Wunspot lives in the one dimensional plane of existence. He can only travel in a straight line, along one radian. He can move 'backwards' or 'forwards' any distance along the straight line, if there is nothing in his path. If there is something in his path he cannot move past it because he has no conception whatsoever of what is meant by sideways movement or vertical movement.

Fig.1

Wunspot's world is restricted to one line (or radian) only

Wunspot stands in line all his life. Because Wunspot is conditioned to the limitations of 'straight-lining', he finds it virtually impossible to imagine an existence in two or more dimensions.

Tooway is a two dimensional being. Tooway has evolved to the awareness, and the restrictions, of two dimensions existing concurrently. Tooway has width although he has no height. He exists on what we humans would consider to be a flat surface or flat plane. Tooway can travel around other two dimensional beings to his heart's content. He can move along radians in any direction in the flat plane, overtaking or turning at will.

Tooway thinks he is in a perfect world, compared to a one dimensional life. However, he has no idea that height – a third dimension that could be added to his existence – would bring undreamed of advantages to his life. So, like Wunspot, he lives within the strict limitations he imposes upon himself.

Fig.2

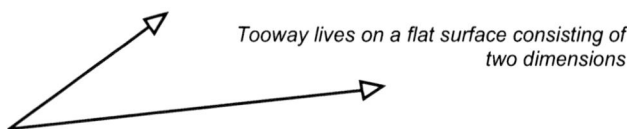

Tooway lives on a flat surface consisting of two dimensions

Threedee has risen to the dizzy peak of knowing that height, added to the dimensions of length and width, produces volume, solid matter and vertical movement.

Yes, it's you and I who live in the solid world of three dimensions. We're all Threedees. Like Tooway and his cohorts, we're caught up in what we see as massive advantages of our limited-dimensional existence compared to a lower-dimensional existence. But we seldom give a thought to the inexplicable advantage that we could bring to ourselves by adding one more dimension to our existence, or to how this can be achieved by a realignment of our thinking mechanism.

Fig.3

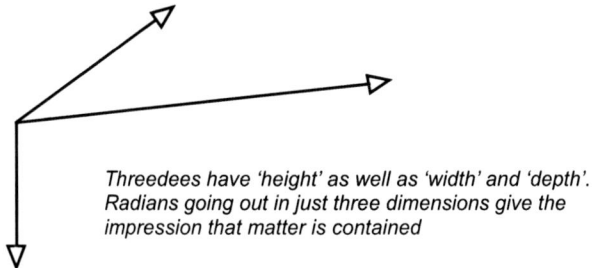

Threedees have 'height' as well as 'width' and 'depth'. Radians going out in just three dimensions give the impression that matter is contained

Threedees can of course move over objects as well as around them. They think that 1,000 miles per hour is highly advanced travel. But they think that going from one side of the universe to the other side in a few milliseconds is an impossible dream. Like Wunspot and Tooway, they consider that to bring added dimension ideas into play is ridiculous.

So, Threedees live their lives crawling around and through solid matter in three-dimensional space.

Threedees acquire things and attach themselves mentally to other objects in an attempt to make their lives acceptable within the three dimensional sphere. These three-dimensional objects include people, animals, plants and mineral based products, which they term their 'property'. Paradoxically, in a three dimensional sphere such as our world, all matter is changing and therefore cannot last. Threedees therefore live lives of much suffering when the objects of their desires change, move away or expire from the three dimensional sphere.

Many Threedees' lives are a struggle, brought about by their fenced-in spiral of individual thinking. As a result of being surrounded by so much 'stuff', they are not able to un-attach themselves from the idea that the three dimensional state is the ultimate form of existence. They want the solid state to be permanent but of course this can never be accomplished.

Even those Thredees who manage to acquire much material stuff only find very temporary satisfaction. Most of them are so caught up in trying to pad out their impermanent little life (here) that they fail to grasp the supremacy that life holds for them if they given a little attention to extra-dimensional abilities, which are very simple to effectuate.

Threedees are in the same trap as Wunspots and Tooways, simply because they fail to look beyond the dense constrictions of their limited existence.

Fourray, whose name is derived from four-ray, lives in four-dimensional state. Four-dimensional existence is easy to understand. Look back at the diagrams of one-dimensional and two-dimensional existences. To add another dimension, in each case, you simply add radians, again, in another direction – at any spot.

If we add an extra radian to either one or two dimensional forms we produce (what we call) 'corners'.

Threedees don't very often conceptualise that they are living a life of corners. They think they are living a life of objects. But they are really living a life of corners, which are limitations occurring as radians go off in three directions. Corners occur at every spot on every object and not just at the end of a straight edge. Corners are not always square either. Neither do they always go off from solid objects at right angles from each other. This makes no difference.

What I mean is if you look at, or run your hand along, the edge of any object you will notice that it is always limited. You always come to the end of it. That's the limitation of three dimensions. Even if you imagine the space of the whole universe to be a three-dimensional object, which it is, you come to the end of it.

(Scientists will soon find the edges of the universe and discover other universes – millions of them – in the third dimension, continually evolving and expiring).

If you add more radians to the limitation of corners you will conceptualise the relative unlimitedness – compared to solid matter – of four dimensions.

Fig.4

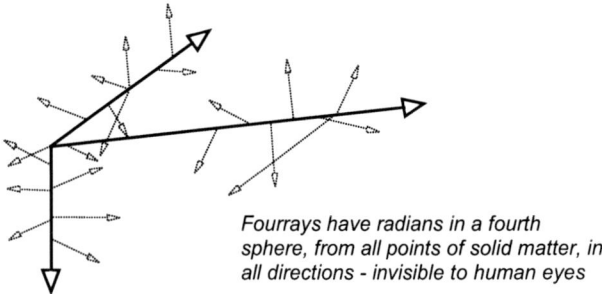

Fourrays have radians in a fourth sphere, from all points of solid matter, in all directions - invisible to human eyes

So, in the one dimensional plane, you simply add one more radian to the single radian to uncover two dimensional existence. You do the same with two-dimensional existence to realise three-dimensional existence. You do the same again in three-dimensional existence to discover four-dimensional existence, and so on, ad infinitum.

The extra radians are unlimited in the fourth dimension even though my diagrams, and my explanation regarding corners, have graphically depicted only a few.

At every single point in the three-dimensional existence there are radians going off in a fourth plane, smaller than the eye or the tiniest measuring instrument can detect. This added plane of existence appears, from a diagram, to go 'outward' from what we see as solid matter but it also goes inward. Scientists call this phenomenon the String Theory.

This may be getting a little more difficult to appreciate than adding dimensions to the lives of Wunspot and Tooway. However, the principle is exactly the same. So, if you have a problem getting your head around this theory, go back to the start of the story and look at how Wunspot and Tooway had the same problem. We can see that Wunspot and Tooway restrict themselves by not opening up to new possibilities of consciousness. Therefore they remain constricted until they do.

In the same way, a four-dimensional mind can see that Threedees are restricting themselves to limited consciousness.

In recent times, Threedees have acquired a little inclination about the possibility of overcoming three dimensional barriers.

Here on earth, for example, we have conquered telegraphy and broadcasting without wires, the use of superconductors that offer no resistance, Kirlian photography which depicts vibrations around and within physical objects – to name but a few achievements. Moreover, sub-atomic science has revealed that solid matter is moving energy which, in dense (slow) vibrational stance simply has the appearance of being more solid than when in a high vibrational stance.

So, in scientific terms we have reached the point of agreeing that the next higher dimension (from us) is a higher vibrational reality than we can perceive around us using the five senses.

Fourrays would not conceive of limiting themselves to three-dimensional life, just as we refuse to entertain the idea of restricting ourselves to two-dimensional life.

One further step is needed to make our appreciation complete. Fourrays, because they are not limited to a tight framework, are not limited to shape but they still have vague form. They are energy like everything else. However, Fourrays are more powerful an energy than us because they are not subject to physical restrictions.

Fourrays can rearrange stuff in the third dimension without much effort just as Threedees can rearrange two-dimensional stuff. It's just that Fourrays can do their thing with much less effort than Threedees because they're not restricted to physics.

Furly is the name I have ascribed to the fifth dimensional being. I concocted this name from combining Five and Curly. It is going to be a bit more difficult for us Threedees to imagine adding radians to a fourth dimensional energy with which we have not yet come to terms. What happens in the fifth dimensional sphere is less limiting again, than in the fourth dimension. Time and space almost disappear and the concept of individuality is so vague as to be unnoticeable.

The radians that are added to Fourrays, to bring about Furlys, are not necessarily in straight lines. That's why I've brought in the idea of 'Curly'. In the vaguer but increasingly powerful higher dimensions, the straight line concept is so vast that it gets (what we perceive as) distorted. Higher dimensions 'curl back' on themselves. This is the reason why everything existent – in all dimensions together – is here and now.

Many more even subtler dimensions exist. Each higher stage is less restrictive and more powerful than the previous. At the highest dimension, all separation is overcome. That is why, in actuality, we are all 'one'.

In truth, you can't count the presence of dimensions in numbers at all. Numbers are a three dimensional (existence) invention. The whole process of what we perceive as moving from one dimension into another is a matter of degree. The reason for this is because the process of reaching higher dimensions is not done in physical steps. It is a matter of the unfoldment of consciousness. However, our three dimensional perception prefers to think in numbers so I have kept to this principle.

What is obvious to us, however, is that any being existing in a constricted dimensional form who can adopt the power of a higher dimensional form, can gain formidable advantage over fellow beings who ignore the higher vibrational benefits. The advantages show themselves to beings like us in personal acumen, control over one's destiny and in knowledge of higher truths.

The reality of this tale

I conceived of this tale, for the benefit of non scientific minds, in order to simplify the appreciation of limited dimensional existence and to understand what can be expected from adding more dimensions to our consciousness. This point is probably obvious to the reader already.

The whole focus here is that one and two dimensions do seem, to us, to exist within the three dimensional make-up. Why is this so?

If you take a cube of any material you can say that any of the six flat planes are two dimensional. However – and here comes the crunch – the two-dimensional surface does not exist on its own. Each two-dimensional surface is part of the cube couldn't possibly exist alone because they have no thickness with which to define them as a stand alone reality. Therefore two dimensions is just a reference. We say the cube has height, width and depth, but each of those factors, or any two of them, cannot exist without the third.

For the same reason, one dimension does not exist on its own either. It is just a reference point.

Can you therefore see, at least as a hypothesis, how the three-dimensional existence, which you think is real, is not a total existence in itself either? The three dimensional state is just a reference point within the four-dimensional. The four-dimensional state is just a reference point within the five-dimensional – and so on. Accordingly, every sphere of consciousness is a limitation of whole consciousness.

Just as you can feel the surface of the cube and know it has no reality without the third dimension being present, you can also feel every solid object and know that it doesn't exist on its own because it is part of the make up – an identifier – of a greater dimensional existence. Therefore, three dimensions – as with any other limited dimensional sphere – is a fragmentation of actuality. String Theory confirms this fact.

I want to spell this out again. I cannot over-emphasise this all important fact. *Each limited dimensional existence is but an identifier. This identification enables the limited dimensional mind to perceive, and move on to, a greater reality.*

The ultimate reality is One-ness, which has no counterpart with which to relate, in its pure form. One-ness identifies itself only via manifestation.

This is not philosophical hogwash. Science has identified these facts. When you look at them objectively, these revelations are no more surprising than the discovery, only a few centuries ago, that the world is spherical and not flat.

Now, science has also recognized that between ten and twenty dimensions are existent in every particle.

You can therefore verify, from nothing else than the simple truths depicted here, that the one and only reality comes about only when you have all dimensions at your disposal. This I refer to as the multi-dimensional existence.

So, we have confirmed that multi-dimensional existence is the one actuality. Moreover, science, at the end of 20th century, has postulated M Theory, which validates the multi-dimension-ness of our existence. The 'multiverse', as it is has been referred to by some scientists, culminates in a boundary-less condition.

Why does the multi-dimensional existence, the one pure consciousness, break itself down into so many pieces?

When you experience pure, multi-dimensional, con-sciousness – which is a practical thing to do – you can (thereafter) conceive of a natural process that has happened. One-ness, the multi-dimensional self, has manifested itself. And this has occurred because one-ness has to identify itself, and it cannot do so in its pure form, which is one without another. Therefore, without intention or effort, as naturally as a flower gives off fragrance, *manifestation comes about consisting of limited containments gradually cascading down from total consciousness.* Hence the restrictions of various degrees of limited consciousness exist.

You might think that identifying the one pure consciousness is the exclusive right of mystics. This is not so. Countless folk like you and I have glimpses of this whole state of being, sufficient to confirm its existence and its qualities. Anyone can do this, if their mind is sufficiently quietened.

Whether you accept this or not, science and mystical knowledge has now come to the same answer – that three dimensional stuff is severely limited and has greater depths. These depths are ignored by most folk during daily life. But they are there and they are easily accessible.

Mankind has not always been in this ignorance. The consciousness of these depths – or heights if you prefer – was once used all the time. That is, before our minds went down a route which blocked off the use of most of our brain cells.

Limited consciousness, such as mankind uses now, is not natural. Unlimited consciousness is natural, not supernatural.

We will explore, under various other headings, why we spend such an extended amount of time in limited consciousness, how we can rid ourselves of all limitations – to tremendous advantage in life – and how we are all on an evolutionary path returning to total consciousness which is our inbuilt desire because we are continually drawing ourselves to a state of total satisfaction, a state of wholeness.

So what we have – what exists in actuality – is a multi-dimensional one-ness. The three dimensions, in which individuals perceive themselves to be contained, are fragments of the whole.

Each limited dimension is like a mirage. Yet in lower-dimensional existence – this one included – we treat our restricted life as real and we think of expanded consciousness as the mirage (that could possibly exist but might not).

What we can do, in order to rectify our ignorance, is de-restrict our consciousness. Thus we can at least prove to ourselves that a whole existence prevails. That's why more and more people are availing themselves of what is referred to as expanded consciousness, via the various 'yogas'.

The state of knowingness I am referring to is the natural consciousness that all human beings had before today's restricted consciousness evolved, over hundreds of millennia.

We have effectively been living in the dark ages. But the latter half of the 20th century witnessed the beginning of the Aquarian Age and a massive change in perception is under way. Thank goodness!

The multi-dimensional, or highest, consciousness is the real you. It is the whole you. It is available to you – accessible now and at every moment. Your attachment to restricted dimensional activity is what veils your appreciation of oneness. However, those who have already regained *full* consciousness – referred to as self-realised beings – can travel the universe in milliseconds and can enter the state of highest consciousness at will. And, as far-fetched as this may sound, it's really nothing special.

As soon as you cease to insist that solidity is our base reality, your consciousness starts to expand. And, in experiencing even the tiniest hint of expanded awareness it is possible to conclude, to re-cognise, that consciousness is the reality of life and what actually exists is an eternal continuum. With this recognition comes the acceptance that life is not just the appearance and disappearance of each little speck of cosmic dust, whether it is a cell, a human being, a rock, a gas, a planet or a universe.

We gain this awareness to some degree as soon as we take on the new viewpoint in our mind. By continually thinking from a wholeness-of-existence perspective, we open up new vistas of understanding. Later, we will discuss practical techniques that align us with our inner vast potential.

Individuality

Most people are convinced of some sort of life hereafter. In the way the mind of a living human would analyse it, we say there are forms of life 'higher' than this life.

But what we think of as a hereafter is human mind projection which has its basis in individualism and separateness.

Using the limitedness of the human mind, we think in terms of each particle, each person, or any other touchable item, as being separate from the other. We therefore project that one day, after death, we have to transform into another type of individual, separate from others, who carries on to another (unknown) life.

This brings about concern in us, ranging from a little trepidation to extreme fear. The result of this is the taboo we still carry with us. We reject deep discussion of life after death because we think the loss of our solid body is a chilling prospect. Leaving our near and dear ones and moving on to a strange environment doesn't bear too much contemplation for the majority of us either.

On this subject there is good news. Each level of existence is a thought process. If you are convinced that you will become a fully fledged individual again when you pass over, in some sort of trouble-free world or heaven, you will do so. I will explain later how most people do this, for a limited period of time. So, don't fear that anyone is going to ask you to drop your individual identity when you are not ready to do so.

In the second chapter of this book we will discuss what happens after 'death'. There is no need to be afraid of anything after this life ends. The afterlife has been named heaven because it is sublime compared to this life.

You may of course already have some desire to let go of the 'little me' feeling (you have on this Earth) and progress to some higher form of existence. Wittingly or unwittingly, you make these decisions while you are here, and nobody else and no invisible power makes them for you. The current limitations on your growth potential are fixed by you and you can change, to evolve at a different pace, if you want to.

Your future as an individual is measureless compared to the brief interlude that is referred to as one lifetime. And this little lifetime is going to be over very soon. So why not plan now for your future? A little bit of open discussion is more likely to lighten your fears rather than deepen them, especially after acquiring some *wholeness* knowledge by means of exploiting your inner access hatch, which is easy to open.

Despite the advice in the paragraphs above, I do *not* advise anyone to seek knowledge in seclusion in preference to living normal daily life. Daily life is the greatest teacher!

Although you create your own individuality, you cannot walk away from the concept of individuality if you still need it in an evolutionary sense. Your future rebirths on Earth, or a similar plane, are inevitable – although the lessons you will face are chosen by you. It's what Gururaj refers to as a choiceless choice.

Everything in the universe(s), in all dimensional spheres, operates in absolute precision with regard to its evolutionary progress. What you can do is to improve your lot, lessen your burdens and fears, fit yourself out with a restored present and an elevated future and control your destiny more competently within the universal laws that apply.

However, if you are presently feeling that you would like to get away from individualism because you are basically fed up with life and its experiences, due to currently having a bad deal or distress, then you are trying to swim against the tide.

Bad deals and negative feelings have to be worked out before you can progress to the smoother, less disturbed states. Fortunately, this can be assisted by using various techniques.

In other words you cannot commit spiritual suicide just because you are down in the dumps. That is impossible. You cannot get away from *karma by jumping off the merry-go-round – even by using physical suicide. You cannot side-step experiences that are only possible to have in these stretched out zones of existence such as Earth life. You move away from *karma by understanding how your mind works and by re-arranging your perceptions.

(*See glossary and chapter 3. Imagine karma to be an inner energy in you needing to be balanced.)

There will come a time in your evolution where you no longer need individuality because of your progression. To be able to understand this you will need to be able to perceive the difference between your readiness and your desire for progress.

So, your individuality is created by your mind and by your inner need to overcome it. How the mind conceives its framework and its subjects and objects will be explained under the heading How the Mind Works.

What Actually Exists? Do *We* Exist?

The infinite life within us never dies. Once that infinite, pure consciousness within us is realised (re-cognised) we have absolute knowledge that death of our actual energy form is an erroneous concept.

How is this realised? It becomes known by the inevitable recollection (one day, whether you desire it or not) that you are actually existence itself – and nothing else. This recollection just happens, unexpectedly. It is a dawning.

At this point you recollect an absoluteness that you (already) know. In that moment you are instantly able to confirm to yourself that you have always been aware of an ever present *actuality* – in every nanosecond of your life – and that you have veiled it from surface consciousness because you got involved with the illusion of individuality.

You will concurrently recognise that this absoluteness is closer to you than your skin, that this absoluteness applies to everything in existence, that there is no such phenomena as separateness and that this life is a minuscule idea, superimposed on what is real.

Furthermore, the (re)cognition of actuality enables you to distinguish clearly that the human mind is so constructed that it can never know this reality. You perceive that it is not the individual 'you' that is recognising this absoluteness. What you realise is that IT itself recognises itself and nothing else does – and IT is what you really are. IT does not recognise mind and mind does not recognise IT. With just a glimpse of this reality, you are momentarily without doubt that this personal worldly existence is conjured up in 'mind'.

I am speaking from direct experience. A countless number of people on Earth, during every generation, get glimpses of actuality. Some are genuine spiritual giants and others are simply in the process of awakening. I, like most others, am in the process of awakening. There are only seven spiritual giants – true Masters – existent on Earth at any point in time. I am simply one of the seekers who has (identified that he has) glimpsed reality and who still has a goodly bundle of mind-stuff to iron out. The Masters can enter pure consciousness at will.

The (re)cognition of our pure consciousness should not to be confused with bliss. I'll describe bliss later on, rather than get away from the subject of existence at this stage.

Whether or not you experience one-ness while you are embodied has no bearing on your progress or your potential. As a matter of interest, each of us brings into daily consciousness the experience of IT – absolute pure consciousness – at the cusp between the sleeping state and the waking state. Yes, we know IT so well. The human mind stifles these conscious recollections because, each time we awake, our minds start up by demanding sensory input.

I have referred here to our one actual consciousness – the one infinite source – as IT. There are many names for IT and most of these I have used or will be using in this book – such as 'pure consciousness', 'divinity', 'non-separateness', the 'infinite energy', the 'impersonal god', 'actuality', 'oneness', the 'Real Self'. Gururaj and other Masters often shortcut all the descriptive names and phrases by referring to the one infinite source as IT. But the other descriptive word terms still prevail and are used invariably for the same purpose.

So, IT exists, has always existed and will always exist. IT is omnipresent, omniscient and omnipotent. That is why we say that life itself is everlasting. The IT, which is our Self, can never be extinguished.

The nature of IT is to manifest, just as flowers give off fragrance – without any conscious effort. But what we need to recognise is when IT manifests, IT also remains IT. The manifestation takes place concurrently, as if on parallel tracks. When you become enlightened you will realise this. From our relative viewpoint we can say that IT has to have some way of confirming its existence. From the viewpoint of IT there is no manifestation, because it is one and therefore does not experience duality. Only from the viewpoint of mind does anything appear to have manifested.

Therefore the (re)cognition of IT is not a recognition that comes from the deciphering process of the mind as we know it. When you glimpse IT you have momentarily gone beyond the mind and allowed your purest subtle consciousness to prevail. True understanding, of what I have tried to depict in the previous few paragraphs, then falls into place.

Each speck of the manifestation is making its way back to the oneness in a process of gradual realisation. This process is called nature.

There are many ways of saying that IT has to manifest itself. But this is really a waste of words. IT is *known* and the *universal mind is *known*, in our consciousness, but this knowledge is beyond all description. All that can be usefully said is a natural manifestation occurs without design, desire or effort. The manifestation erupts, expands and contracts again into its source. We can see this happening to the three-dimensional universe and this is a replication and a reflection of what happens on all (dimensional) levels concurrently.

(**see chapter 2*)

In simple terms, what we are, as individuals, is consciousness in many forms and many dimensions, *including* pure consciousness (IT), which is the source of every object, every action and every thought.

In one sense you could say we do not exist at all – only IT exists, and IT is us and everything else – and that would be true. But our earthly forms are real to us and we have them and our evolution for the purpose of re-realising our reality. Each individual relative-ness is making its way back to the one reality.

What Is Love? What Is God? What Is Truth?

First, I will talk in terms of what love is not. One of my favourite popular musicians, David Gray, wrote, "Honey, if I'm honest, I still don't know what love is."

Popular music has become one of the largest and most lucrative industries in the world, the contents of which are based almost exclusively upon inter-personal emotion, which people refer to as love.

But love is not emotion. What loving partners feel for each other is emotion. What loving partners feel for each other is not love.

So, why are such feelings called love? Feelings are called love because, when emotions become blissful between two people, a euphoric satisfaction is experienced. The positive emotions experienced feel good, causing the human mind to react in a happy and light manner. What happens is that the euphoric state overtakes the intellectual mechanics of the mind allowing more of our inner subtle energy to flow. We become orientated more by feelings and less by logic. This is a higher dimensional experience.

The *source* of you and of all energy, subtle or purely physical, is love. Love is Truth (is God). Love, in its purest sense, is yet another name for pure consciousness (IT), the impersonal infinite energy from which all other energy springs.

Love filters through into emotion indistinctly when you are feeling good. Of course, emotion can knock you down as well as raise you up whereas love – real love – can only elevate you.

To reiterate, love itself is not the feelings and emotions that you experience. These feelings and emotions come from sensory input, as the mind map, shown in the next section, will demonstrate.

Love – pure love – is not involved in sensory input. Love is pure consciousness (located at the opposite end from sensory input on the mind map).

The mind continuously relates to sensory input and memory, and this is what veils pure love. The mind, working in this way, is what causes the emotions. Emotions, feelings and the like are energies rousted up within the framework of the (unreal) mind, based on sensory input, memory *and* ego.

Solutions to your romantic 'love' problems are brought about by de-intensifying your reactions to sensory input. If you become open to the flow of *actual* love, your sensory input and memory combination will start to lose its hold as an overall controller of your physical and mental self. Your negative emotions will thereby weaken, in respect of the hold they have on you.

Until you do get into this more pure flow of energy you will be buffeted around continually by your emotional responses. This buffeting reveals itself as having a 'low' for every 'high'. Sometimes it seems as if there are more lows than highs.

Gururaj used to say that when you fall in love the emphasis in this phrase is that you fall. In the situation where you are besotted with someone, you have become attached because of a weakness rather than strength. The emotions then run high. The answer to this problem is to *elevate* yourself in love rather than fall. This will make a truer and longer lasting love match between any two people.

When you fall in love you eventually get over the fall. Feelings must then emerge on a different basis to establish a permanent relationship. In the true light of day, when the fall is recovered from, many couples find they do not have sufficient common ground to continue a long term partnership.

Gururaj also often voiced the following one of his many familiar phrases to his followers (chelas), "I do not love, I *am* love." When you *become* love you will have risen above the effects of sensory input, memory and ego. Then you live in permanent bliss and there is nothing in the world that can affect you.

When you live in bliss you also live in this moment. When you live in the moment you are not affected by the past or the future. Then your mind, which imagines past and future in order to maintain its existence, ceases to have a hold over you.

As strange as this may sound, living in this moment is an extremely practical proposition. In reality there is no such thing as time, so by living in the moment you are aligning yourself with nature. You can learn a focusing technique, which I later refer to, for helping to live this moment.

Living this moment is a superb experience. You can do it

from time to time or all the time. When you do, you will become focused. Consequently you'll avoid being scattered, thereby eliminating the dilemma of going around in pointless and problematical circles all your life.

By living in the moment you will eliminate 90 per cent of the energy you waste getting nowhere.

Some changes in perspective are required to live 'the here and now'. But the result of doing so is that you cease to project thousands of useless images each day. Chapter 6 of this book refers to this. It is all a case of stripping out your conditioning. This is known as unconditioning. You replace the established 'blocking' thought processes with more useful ones.

Where does God really come in to all this? God is a man-made word depicting the almighty, eternal power of a source from which we stem.

We have just referred to that source as pure love (pure consciousness, IT). But can God and love be one and the same?

There is a saying, 'God is love, is truth'. But this is confusing to the human mind because we pattern ourselves to think that everything in existence, including the ultimate eternalness, which we can't see, is in the form of separate 'things'.

It is this same patterning of the mind that insists on there being a separate being that produces the energy – the love, call it what you like – that is responsible for the birth of the universe.

Simultaneously, it is easy to hand over the ultimate responsibility for our lives to some supreme being who (we might imagine) created everything – albeit those who do so are content that such a being, presumably pictured as being of kind heart, oversees the devastation suffered in many corners of the globe.

It takes just one simple step to sort all this through. The answer is in the acceptance – which is not blind belief because you can prove it for yourself – that all existence is consciousness. Accordingly, you can easily understand that limited spheres of existence, like ours, produce the concept of separateness as an anchor to which our limited minds can relate.

With one glimpse of higher consciousness we can conceptualise the reality of oneness as opposed to separation. We come to the knowledge that God *is* love *is* truth – *is us*. There is no separation. All these words are meaningless. We – our consciousness – are the whole of everything. Yes, each (so called) individual can say, "I am the whole of everything."

How can we accept this fact, take responsibility for it and utilise it to good and great effect in our present life and in our future?

First we need to know how the human mind really works. Unless we understand this, the facts above soon become some sort of fantasy in our memory. When we truly understand the mind we can see its limitations, its illusory status and its folly, all day long. We can move to a more real way of thinking – a more subtle way of thinking. This will bring with it real knowledge instead of belief, as well as untold self-power.

2

Your Perspective

Your Route – Your Potential

How the Mind Works

What is the human mind? The mind cannot be found anywhere, yet it forms the whole of your justification for yourself. Therefore, it rules your life.

Descartes stated, "I think, therefore I am."

This saying attempts to define that without thought the human being is nothing. This is one way of looking at human life. It would be true if mankind could work out the whole of existence based on nothing other than three-dimensional energy. However, mankind cannot do that.

"I am that I am" comes from the highest perspective of all existence, the IT, and from this perspective the individual mind has no foundation. The very highest perspective is beyond the mind.

The individual mind works from sensory input and memory. The ego and the intellect, which are invisible, non-discernable calculators and assessors, juggle the information input by means of minute electrical (energy) impulses, into personally limited judgements which are stored at various levels of recall.

In the diagram, the large rectangle demonstrates how the mind is boxed in. The framework of the mind is a limited structure which tries to justify itself. It is self-made and self-limiting – an individuality that exists within itself only.

Appreciating how the mind really works enables you to utilise the mind to your advantage. This comes about by being

Fig. 5 The mind-works map

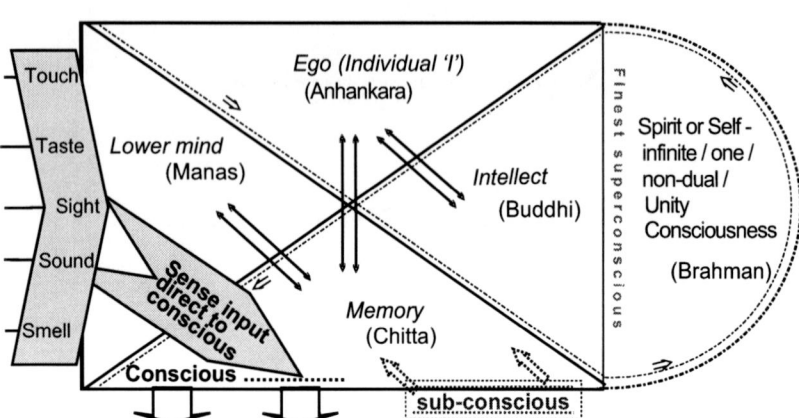

able to reinforce your thinking mechanism with the all-powerful subtle extra-dimensional qualities of your being and of your universal mind. These incredible forces are always present in abundance and totally accessible.

Psychologists and psychiatrists focus on an individual's *closed circuit*, not bringing into account the fact that each conscious mind relies not only on the subconscious but on the anchors of the more subtle minds within.

This statement may have been treated as somewhat heretical in the past. However, now that science has revealed our multi-dimensional make-up, the doubters of these principles are starting to acknowledge their reality.

The diagram demonstrates how the human being is governed mostly by the five senses – seeing, touching, smelling, tasting and hearing. Manas, which is really the conscious mind we use continuously, is influenced by these inputs.

The lower mind cannot function on its own. The impressions in the lower mind are sent to the Chitta, which is the memory box. The deepest part of the Chitta is not immediately subject to conscious recall and we refer to it as the subconscious mind.

Because of the multitude of sensory inputs we have, many

impressions are stored in the subconscious. Yet these impressions activate and motivate our actions – instructed by the conscious mind.

In addition, the conscious mind (Manas) requires identification because there is only a memory box from which images are formed, causing impressions.

The subconscious mind is like a box of pigeon holes where certain files, of every experience, are put. So if you see a dog, that very act of seeing will transmit impulses within the conscious/subconscious mind for comparison – a dog that you have seen before – and only then the recognition occurs that it is a dog. Otherwise you would not know if it's a dog or a cat or a mouse.

This is only the first transmission. The subconscious mind transmits itself to ego or the I, the individual I.

The sensory inputs of the conscious mind transmit to the subconscious for comparison. But after the comparison the mind has to identify itself with the ego sense in order to justify its existence. For without the ego sense, no one could really live. Even the most perfected Master must have two per cent imperfection in him; otherwise he would lose all sense of individuality. He wouldn't be able to eat, sleep or perform any biological function.

Furthermore, the ego sense still requires certain guidance and that comes from the Buddhi which is intellect. The function of the intellect is to weigh the pros and cons. And, weighing the pros and cons, the Buddhi transmits images back to the ego, assessing how information or experience will fit in with your personal individual ego viewpoint.

For instance, you might like chicken. Why? It's because of the various impressions about chicken. The Buddhi analyses it and transmits it to your individual self with its likes and dislikes, and then it gets back to the memory box where it pulls out the file and says, "Ah, this is okay, chicken is fine, curried chicken or roast," or whatever. And that is submitted to the conscious mind where your five senses will start enjoying it.

How can this process be altered? The simple answer is that as the ego is lessened, the value of sensory inputs becomes less too. And by lessening the value of the sensory inputs, you become less attached. You can reach the stage of non-attachment.

Understanding the ego is important. You are probably familiar with associating the ego of a person to be either a means to show off, a means to prefer oneself against others or a means to bolster up a vain, if not false, image.

But the ego I am referring to is much more basic. Each person identifies themselves to be an individual, solid item which assumes that the universe surrounds them and that they have a place which fits in the scheme of things, and that the whole scenario is important.

This is the viewpoint of the average person who insists on living solely the three-dimensional angle of perception because they don't want to, or don't know how to, take on a multi-dimensional standpoint. Most of humanity lives like this.

The ego cannot be destroyed and no attempt should be made to destroy it. We want to *sublimate* the ego – and this sublimation is not dependent on whether a person is vain, powerful or meek, confident or introverted. The ego is important. It has to be honoured. Identification of individuality is highly relevant if you find yourself embodied on this planet because there are lessons to learn by this means.

Honouring the ego does not conflict with lessening the ego. When I say the ego should be lessened I mean it should be clarified. It is like *stretching* the ego so that from a dark mass it becomes opaque, the result of which is to let a little light – or real knowledge – through it. In this way the ego and the effect of sensory input can be surmounted.

The ego is stretched and the effect of sensory input is lessened by partaking in regular yogic practices such as correct meditation. Correct meditation deals with thoughts in such a way that the thoughts do not affect you – for short periods of time. You momentarily go beyond the mind.

You can't obliterate thoughts. That would be the same as trying to annihilate the ego. It's impossible, however hard you try, and the attempt would not be conducive to mastering your mind. But you can get on top of your thought patterns, appreciate them for what they are and deal with them by using a simple mechanism involving thought presence and observation.

Each time you go beyond the thinking mind, using appropriate techniques, a little more of the wholeness of you is filtered through into the conscious mind.

In the diagram the superconscious is represented by a line behind the intellect. The semi-circle to the right represents infinity which contains all knowledge and all consciousness. It is known by one of the many names I have already referred to including pure consciousness or IT. It is also sometimes referred to as the spirit.

The spirit is infinite and eternal and, although you could say it is an individual's spirit, it is also all of existence at the highest level of consciousness. This fact allows us to appreciate that the individual and the eternal oneness are the same. It is only an individual's mind that says, "I am an individual".

It is difficult to show everything beyond the human mind level in one diagram, without over complicating it. Just imagine that the semi circle (to the right) represents everything *beyond* the conscious and sub-conscious mind levels.

A useful tip, in using this mind diagram, is to imagine the limitedness of the mind within the rectangle to be 5 per cent of what we are and the limitlessness represented by the semi-circle to be 95 per cent of what we are. This helps in gaining a clearer perspective of our realness as well as our potential.

These percentage numbers are not accurate. I use these numbers, in a reference context, because scientists currently anticipate that there are up to 20 energy dimensions superimposed on what appears to be three dimensional existence. A 20 to 1 ratio seems to me a practical idea for the sake of our imagination. In actuality there are not numbers of dimensions. Numbers are a worldly counting mechanism. When you move from a lower reality to a higher reality it is a matter of degree. The unrestricted mind encompasses all. Limited mind focuses on limited fragments of the whole, thereby projecting separation, which necessarily incorporates a counting mechanism.

The sensory inputs to the mind are temporary so we need not allow them to affect us, but we do. The main cause of suffering and misery is because we pay so much attention to sensory inputs in the lower mind. The sensory inputs get planted in the subconscious mind in the form of impressions.

If you operate solely on assessment of sensory inputs, when you leave this physical body, the only thing that will go with you are these impressions, these thought forms which can also be called your subtle body, because your subtle body is composed of thought forms. And these thought forms will regulate your next birth.

So if you have mastered your thought processes before you leave this physical body, those thought forms formulate themselves for you to be born again in circumstances which are better for you than if you allow the mind to be your master.

All this is so simple. It's so logical. Why is one child born in totally unhappy circumstances or ill or sick or maimed, while another child is born in wealth, riches and happiness? There is no bearded old man up there dishing out unfairness. It is you yourself, it is your own karma that controls your destiny and your karma is backed up and formulated by the impressions of the subconscious. We'll review how to dispel karma a little later on.

To repeat, the ego self has its own little self-importance. And the ego self cannot be totally destroyed. You find many theologies trying to impress upon people that you must become ego-less. This is an impossibility because if you become ego-less you'll have no recognition of your personality.

It is individuality, which is supported by the ego, which gives you some sense of consciousness. The ego needs refining, not annihilating. And the more refined the ego becomes, the purer the consciousness becomes and the greater the awareness becomes.

Awareness is a thing where you just know. It defies all analysis of the Buddhi, the intellect. You just know. When you are really aware you are *attuned*. This means you have become integrated, with a good deal of your subtle mind operating in you. Then, when you come to a fork in the road you'll just take the correct turn instead of the wrong one because your mind is not such a separate entity to the universal mind.

In reality there's only one mind and your mind is as vast as the entire universe. The reason you have no recognition of its vastness or universality is because of that individualisation of the ego.

By using self-integration practices such as personally prescribed meditation, one-pointedness focusing, subtle energy manipulation, ingesting prana or life-force, etc. together with attunement triggers, we find a greater control of the sensory inputs by which the majority of people are ruled. Refinement takes place throughout the mind mechanism.

There is endless subtle energy permeating you all the time, so why shouldn't you use it to great effect instead of repeating these lifetimes of problems over and over again? The subconscious mind is made up of all kinds of impressions and it needs a good scouring to get you out of the ruts you are in, which you caused by the blockages you have piled up.

The intellect stands in the way of the spirit. When, through meditation and spiritual practices, this intellect is cleared up, it is like a dirty window you clean so you can see through it again. Then the full force of the spirit shines through. You can then use some of the 95 per cent greater energy of your Self that you have been missing out on. And there are so many practical ways in which you can benefit.

As the purer energy shines through, because of its clarity it will destroy the impressions which are darkness. It will stretch the ego. The more energy that shines through, the more transparent the stretched ego becomes. And it all improves together – the ego, the memory and reduction in the effect of the sensory inputs.

So, the mind-works diagram demonstrates that everything is permeated by the spirit. The spirit is your highest consciousness; your most subtle level of being. It goes through every facet of you. The only thing is for us to cognize it, recognise it, realise it and live it, which happens more and more as you gain power over your mind.

The impressions, which cause your limitations, can be largely dispelled. Then your conscious mind will become less burdened and less coloured. You will be more real and more joyful, with a lighter mind, as well as becoming a more potent force regarding your life and your destiny. Right action will become automatic.

What traditional medical science does not yet understand is that to permanently change a tendency in your personality you need to allow your subtle or spiritual energy to infiltrate your mind. It is only by re-cognising a truer perspective of your existence that you can let go of old patternings.

Remember, the base ego is the overriding conviction that 'I am an individual.' This governs the boxed-in conditioning of the mind. But this is a false premise because it does not take into account the multi-dimensional perspective that your inner subtle energy allows.

Consequently, psychoanalysis has its extreme limitations. Analysts help you to appreciate the formulation of your patterning since childhood, to give you a reason for your tendencies. Therapies to address these tendencies can help in relieving the effect of your tendencies. But are tendencies completely eradicated by analysis? I think not.

Tendencies build up over countless lifetimes. Hence we are all born in different circumstances (that are perfect for addressing the tendencies). We have to change the tendencies ourselves if we want a permanent 'cure.' The only way to do this is to allow the superconscious to infiltrate the conscious. This is the perfectly natural reconditioning and revitalising process. In this way, darkness is dispelled. The light grows from dim to bright by turning up the energy source, not by examining the dimness.

The deepest levels of the subconscious mind are vast and patternings are taken from lifetime to lifetime until they are changed at their roots, not at their surface.

The re-activation of your universal Self is the permanent

answer to controlling the human mind. You infiltrate some of the 95 per cent of you that is more or less dormant. It is not a re-activation of the spirit because the spirit is there all the time and so is every other level of subtle energy from the spirit level right down to the level of your boxed in three dimensional (related) mind.

We simply allow higher consciousness in. When higher consciousness is allowed in, it refreshes personal conception, personal acceptance and personal perspective.

The Universal Mind

The idea of a universal mind is not a strange one. Mind generally means *arranged set or arranged form* into which everything fits. There are trillions and trillions of energy motions happening every split second. The universe propels itself and everything fits perfectly and precisely into its confines. This is nature, and it works without instruction or analysis.

In the diagram, the universal mind would correspond with the finest superconscious area which is beyond the intellect and in touch with the spirit – but a manifestation of the spirit rather than the spirit itself.

In actuality there is only one mind and not a lot of separate minds. (See also 'Non-Separation'). The one mind is the universal mind.

I am not talking here of the vast mass of planets rolling around thinking, "I am a universe." That would be how the human mind thinks. The universe(s) are a manifestation(s) and manifestation is pure nature. Nobody designed it and it cannot be stopped or altered. The manifestation comes about by impulses that just occur. We'll examine why this happens later.

The universal mind, or soul, differentiates itself from the spirit. This very process of differentiation is necessary for the universe to remain in motion. The differentiation has to take various forms, through various stratas of existence, until it solidifies itself as an individual mind.

But apart from the individuality that mankind perceives,

there is still this thread running through all those single beads, as the universal mind. So what each individual has to do is to combine the individual mind with the universal mind. Everything in the universe is operating by nature, except for human beings, or similar forms of life, with their veiled perspective. In pure nature, multi-dimensional consciousness is predominant. Nature operates without analysis.

The human mind restricts itself so confinedly. Animals don't block their consciousness. Birds and many other creatures know what weather is coming next week or next month and they have no speech, no television, no barometers or satellites to assist them. Humans were once like this too but have now blocked their consciousness so badly that they have lost almost all of their nature. Humans have allowed themselves to suffer because the ego encourages living by *non-nature*.

Plants and minerals have consciousness too, as with everything else in the lower dimensional planes. Consciousness is like the engine of evolution, fuelled by the natural pure source of energy which all parts of the engine rely upon.

It is mankind that messes things up. Since the moment the first man or woman looked at his or her reflection and said, "I am *something*, therefore I will comfort myself (e.g. by means of power over others and by stockpiling material stuff)," then mankind started to suffer dissatisfaction and fear of death. The feeling of being separate then increased and increased until unity consciousness became blocked out.

Here is the basis of all suffering within mankind. It is the unseen existence, the 95 per cent consciousness human beings block out that can resolve every problem in the human scheme. It is this 95 per cent of consciousness, which is counterpart to every cell of physical existence, which science is now validating. Recent discoveries, resulting from sub-atomic investigation, hold the answers to previously unsolved mysteries.

Science also wants to know why things happen in the first place, but they can never discover why the universes started by measuring on the physical plane, if the hypotheses are based on limited consciousness.

The universal mind is an actuality and each individual can verify this for themselves. You cannot get a greater scientific confirmation than this. We are talking *actuality* here. We are talking of certainty and not numbers or amounts, which are changeable and therefore inaccurate.

Science has previously operated from the basis of something, somewhere, having been created. The new view of multi-dimension-ness has already changed the opinion of many who previously believed in a single controlling power-entity, to accepting that manifestation is an ongoing process rather than a design.

Another fact that can be experienced in higher consciousness will undoubtedly be helpful in scientific research. It is this: the universe expands, remains static and then implodes at the ratio of 1:4:2. This fact is also useful to us in our quest to uncondition the mind. One of several balance and stillness practices I recommend is designed to re-align us with our subtle and spiritual energies, by using this pulsation of the universe.

How Your Subtle Mind Works

In trying to gain advantage from re-activating our sense of universal-ness, we essentially have to start with the little self as a servile tool. We are in effect trying to awaken ourselves from a dream.

In the case of an ordinary dream we awake automatically. In the case of awakening from the illusion that we are three-dimensional beings, we have to become proactive. We have to solve this illusion for ourselves. There is no guide who can do it for us. Even the enlightened masters can only throw light on the path. We have to do the walking.

The little self of you includes your body, but it is mostly the mind – represented by the rectangle in the diagram. The universal self comprises our 95 per cent hidden consciousness and hidden power, which we want to access.

What is frequently referred to as the subtle mind is the combination of both aspects. In other words, the subtle mind is the individual mind re-activated by the infusion of any amount of the infinite subtle energy store within.

Put another way, the subtle mind is your earthly mind infused with a predominance of natural, subtle energy as opposed to your mind as it was when you relied solely on sensory input and memory logic. The greater the amount of inner subtle energy you open up to, the more subtle your mind becomes. The more subtle your mind becomes, the less limited you become and the more you are self-directed by the nature of you rather than the false superimposition you have conjured up because of ego orientation.

I want to delineate that the spirit is beyond all mind and all form. The spirit is the power, the essence from which everything springs – called by any name you wish to use – whereas the subtle mind is a utility for assisting the individual.

The spirit can be called upon. You do this by employing your own effort and focus. The spirit empowers the whole process but it does not consciously come to your aid. The spirit is not pro-active. The spirit does not have a mind. The spirit knows nothing of separation. Therefore it knows nothing either of space or objects, by which we human beings sense we are surrounded. The spirit is pure, untainted, non-dual.

I also want to clarify one further point. Do not confuse the subtle mind with the subtle body, to which I will refer later (see Exactly What Happens After Death). The subtle body is the term used for the ethereal you that carries on after the physical body is dropped and is a mental self untainted by sensory input or lower-dimensional restriction.

Subtle Mind Potency

The benefits of utilising the subtle mind are too numerous to describe. But the power to control your life and your destiny by using higher consciousness is unquestionable.

Once you start to live by means of a more subtle mind you will wonder how you could have lived your life before without doing so.

First there are the practical benefits of bringing about changes that you desire in your attitude, your environment, your confidence, your lifestyle etc. Secondly, there can be a massive reduction in stress and suffering. Thirdly, you can bring yourself almost anything from a parking space to a spouse; from prosperity to better health; from happiness to sublime bliss.

An additional (and optional) reward, if you want to refine your mind to the finest degree, is that you can re-discover the consciousness of your Real Self. This may not be your personal goal at this moment in your evolution. You do not have to use or pursue this final endeavour. The more practical benefits I have already mentioned can be exploited without any deep interest in higher consciousness or pure consciousness. But, certainly, the more you reveal your true self, the more joyful life will become.

The more that nature is allowed to be operating in you, the smoother your path becomes. You will also, having taken an interest in your Real Self during this lifetime, retain this patterning in your evolution.

As you will glean from the final chapters of this book, desired changes in your life can come overnight or over a much longer term, dependent upon how much you choose to cling to your old limited patterning and at what rate you are prepared to uncondition yourself. Whatever the rate of change, benefits will come. I have witnessed evidence of this from my encounters with thousands of people who brought subtle energy into their daily lives.

I emphasise again – there are no beliefs involved in exploiting your subtle mind. Neither will the process affect any belief you wish to retain, be it religious or otherwise.

Unconditioning is both the process and the upshot of using subtle energy. It is not reconditioning. Unconditioning is untwisting. Reconditioning is untwisting followed by twisting up again in a different pattern.

You can recondition your mind as you wish, if you wish. You take on what you want and you dump what you want to dump. Unconditioning is simply opening yourself up to the flow of your own greater nature, which you have been blocking with the incessant spiralling activity of the locked-in mind.

Why Death Is Not Our Finality

All your life you are honing in on your final moment. But are you prepared for this inevitable event?

Most people refuse to contemplate their death, despite the inevitability of it being the *only* certainty in life.

No wonder our evolution is slowed down on this planet! Human beings generally don't attempt to find out what death is all about. Consequently they don't discover what life is all about either.

Few people grasp the concept of the purpose of life in its true perspective. Few have certain knowledge of any consciousness that exists after the body is shed. So they rely on belief or gut feeling. It is not surprising there is so much fear in humankind. Fortunately, there is light at the end of the tunnel.

Most of us tend to put off thinking about death until very late in life. When the body starts to show signs of degradation at say, the 50 to 60 years age range, thoughts of old age start to creep in. By the 60 to 70 years age range the body feels older so thoughts of death are forced to the forefront. Yet most thoughts about death, even at that stage, are concerned with trying not to think about it!

Some folk, rather than fear being permanently asleep, worry about how they will be judged after death or how they will get on in a possibly uninviting, strange land of spiritual beings.

You may even try to console yourself with the idea that the afterlife will be acceptable because everyone else has gone there before – and that religious top-knobs have assured everyone for eons that the land of milk and honey awaits – unless we have been bad, when it will be a land of fire and brimstone!

What you really need to know is the truth and then you will not be scared at all. Nor will you need to listen to anyone other than yourself. If you are not scared of death, you will be freer in life and get much more out of it.

We view our death as the end of life. We feel sorry for other people who die because we think that they might have stayed here a bit longer.

I will attempt to explain, even if I don't convince you right away, that an early death does not take anything away from an individual. Moreover, there is no actual death but just a temporary cessation of the restricted consciousness we bestow on ourselves in these lower dimensions.

Life is a continuum which is not dependent on being embodied in the physical plane. Life and death of the body is an illusory superimposition.

All this philosophy and knowledge does not prevent pain in you when a beloved one passes on. The suffering caused by sudden loss is inevitable after a dear one departs. It is necessary to grieve because it is not healthy to keep feelings locked away. The limited mind needs to process its feelings if it is not to incur further blockages.

With a more subtle perspective predominating in us, we are assisted in imagining our lives coming and going like the new leaves on a tree each year. That's a pertinent analogy because, like all nature, we are not meant to be here forever. The seasonal changing format of trees is one of the most treasured examples of our love of nature. We watch the leaves fall and celebrate their colours and the scene as a whole. Then we clean up the decayed matter and think of the new life soon to appear with the advent of spring. You can think of other analogies, I'm sure, as examples of our lives being in tune with nature.

I have a favourite extract from The Buddha which may help you, as it has helped me, over the loss of a loved one.

"These children and riches are mine" – thinking thus the fool is troubled. Since no one even owns himself, what is the sense in thinking *my* children (or loved ones) and *my* riches? Verily, it is the law of humanity that, although one accumulates thousands of worldly goods, one still succumbs to the spell of death. All hoardings will be dispersed; whatever rises will be cast down; all meetings must end in separation.

UDANAVARGA 1.20–22

This type of perspective helps us to think in terms of a wholeness of existence rather than treating the demise of each individual as a permanent tragedy. Each individual, passing on, goes back to nature; the natural process we all undergo, without resistance, after each few decades of three-dimensional consciousness.

When a person dies, celebrate their time on Earth. They have done what they can do. Then they have gone to a most peaceful and deserved rest where the mind is not continually nagging at them. They are in a semi-blissful state preparing for a new life opportunity.

Exactly What Happens After Death?

Do not fear leaving the body. It is not a scary experience. To the contrary, it is going to be the most sublime experience of your life!

After a person dies, what happens to them? He or she sheds their physical body as we all know. But the human system, as well as anything and everything else, has not just one self, it has three selves. The physical self is the first component. Secondly, there is subtle self which is the mental body, and thirdly, there is that which empowers it all, the spiritual body.

You cast off the physical body like you cast off old garments, but the subtle body carries on.

The subtle body is the repository of all the experiences you have gained until the moment of parting, not only of this lifetime but of all the lives that your individual-ness has lived since the primal atom.

The subtle body or soul is the mental body and contained within it is the spiritual body. The two aspects of you that remain after shedding the physical body – the subtle and spiritual – will be operating in higher dimensions.

So the subtle body goes on and carries forth with it the impressions gained from the experiences the individual undergoes. These impressions are known as samskaras. Your subtle body is nothing else but a bundle of samskaras. These samskaras underpin the mind's framework and play a huge part in moulding you as a person when you are in the physical body.

In the mental (subtle) body the power of intellect is still alive. The power of discrimination is still alive but it becomes unfettered, unchained from the physical body and it functions, after the body is shed, at a far purer level.

So what have you really lost? You have only put aside the confused, discontent, imperfect part of yourself. The physical body is an encumbrance, like a weight we carry around.

The subtle body, drawing more power from the spiritual body and finding more clarity, can evaluate your situation more clearly.

At the moment of death, when the subtle body is released, then, being closer to the source, the various layers of consciousness in the subtle body automatically function as a Unity.

These layers are (a little) memory of the ordinary conscious mind, the total memory of the sub-conscious mind and its various levels plus the super-conscious mind. Having shed the physical body, you no longer use up the energies of the mental body that were wasted on sensory reaction and which were so fragmenting to you, causing your potential power and your potential happiness to be restricted.

When you do meditation and other subtle energy practices you withdraw from the senses but you also have thought patterns in the way. The difference, after the body is dropped, is that you become oblivious of the physical; the subtle body can thereby function at its maximum level without effort and without the confusion caused by the conscious mind.

At the moment of death, the sub-conscious and the super-conscious and the memories of the conscious gather together into a much heightened state of vibration (which is experienceable here, in the body, if you integrate yourself).

In this heightened state of vibration every memory of this life becomes alive and you can see from the time of birth until the time of leaving your body. Everything flashes by sequentially in a panoramic view. But you see it in two different aspects. You see it sequentially – linearly – and at the same time you see it as wholeness.

This experience, in timelessness, becomes accessible because you momentarily capture the zenith of the universal mind. That high consciousness is virtually impressionless, so the reality of non-time comes to the fore and you experience that everything is here and now.

But your samskaras go with you.

You cannot settle in that impressionless sphere. The total here and now concept does not last and you settle yourself at the level of dimensional experience that your evolution allows.

Then your journey begins. It is a joyous journey. In the subtle state, the mental body experiences greater joy because it is closer to the real all-pervading spiritual self. So the moment of death is joyous – something never ever to be feared.

Joy *can* be experienced here and now, by partaking in correct meditation, contemplation and spiritual practices that take you, quite naturally, beyond the body and beyond your little conscious mind. You can dive into the realms beyond the conscious mind and feel the joy permeating there; when you can *experience* that after death there is nothing but joy.

What is also highly pertinent (to the content of this book) is that you can, here and now, condition your experiences that will occur immediately after you pass on.

Any thought can be materialised and it can be materialised much more so in the subtle state of existence. For example, if you are very faithful to a belief that after death you are, say, going to live in a mansion and be surrounded by objects and people of your choice – you will get these in an experiential way in your mental (subtle) body.

Likewise, if you instill in your mind, now, that life after death is joyful, you will experience that joy. The only difference is that you can easily form a mental picture of a mansion and beautiful objects because you can see them. Joy is a more subtle experience. It is not from the sensory input.

The mind can project itself into a different dimension and often does so. This has been verified during near death experiences. Because the mind has deep implanted memories of, say, a late relative, within this projection you could conjure up that person or persons and in that dimension you find them to be a reality. But, in truth, it is nothing else than a projection. You find these sorts of experiences referred to in books that report of connections with the dead.

That is why mediumship should not be encouraged. The mechanics of mediumship are all projections, which are not reality. The experiences described are not real after-life experiences. They are mind conditionings. The medium is not a spiritual supremo. Mediums are dabbling – in a very low area in the next dimension – and are soaked in mind stuff like everyone else.

I would not have anything to do with such unreality if I were you, because you can easily be misguided by the conditioning of someone else's mind, regardless of their good intentions.

That is not what you need and it is not what the person playing the medium needs. It may temporarily satisfy your mind or your broken heart or your loneliness, but you should try to rise above that. What is more, you can find every answer within yourself if you go about it in the right way.

You are responsible for yourself and to yourself. Why belittle that position? If you find a connection to *other sources*, you would be well advised to try to sublimate it. Don't scatter it on to others because it is coloured with your mind conditioning.

Some mediums claim their audible source to be the spirit. This is not true. The spirit is pure consciousness. The spirit is one and not dual, and cannot speak words or have ideas or impressions of people or universes or any other various-dimensional stuff. Mediumship is of the individual mind. I call it *mindiumship*.

Joy, which is a real and natural experience, has nothing to do with your samskaras and it has nothing to do with the human concept of heaven and hell. Heaven and hell are here on Earth.

With your projections you can also create heaven and hell in another realm, if you want to, by sticking faithfully to that idea. Keep on believing that you are going to burn in the fires of hell and you are going to burn. Keep on believing that it's going be joyful on the other side and that very mental conditioning that you are undergoing will make it joyful.

Yes, as many readers might be thinking, it could be a kind of self-hypnosis. It could be a sort of brain-washing in yourself that certain thoughts will materialise on the subtler plane. It is all nothing but projections caused by your conditioning.

So, the truth of the matter is that in the subtle state, when you have dropped the body, you do not have this encumbrance of the body with you. You are closer to the spirit. And the nature of the spiritual life is nothing but bliss and joy and you can feel it more intensely without a body.

The subtle mind is much more powerful than the conscious mind. Consequently, any projection you insist on taking with you when you die will be intensified while you hang on to it. Therefore, project joy and not fear.

If you are fearful in this life you will project such thoughts forward and give yourself a future life that tests your fear again until you stop being fearful. You must rise to joy eventually so why not do it now?

Here I should briefly mention the subject of suicide. Despite your moment of death being joyful, it is not positive to take your own life. Most people committing suicide cannot bear this life any longer. A few also do it because their minds are filled up with the euphoria of the 'spirituality' of less burdensome spheres that await us. These two reasons have the same basis – getting out of this life. But, while you are in your present body, there are lessons to be learned. There are steps forward to take that can only be taken in this sphere. Taking your own life will possibly cause a retrograde step in your evolution, whereas working at enjoying life, especially during a period when it is not enjoyable, will have a positive result.

Whatever your circumstances are in this life you will quickly make a better life using positivity all the time. This will lead you to some joy of life while in this body. If you die feeling joy and not fear you will benefit so much. The feelings that you take with you form the basis of the blueprint for your next life (or lives) as soon as you pass over.

I have experienced both fear and negativity. Therefore I

know how difficult it is to engender positivity when all seems pointless. All I can say, to those who are feeling down, is that improvement will *always* come from remaining determined when you're convinced that determination is slipping away from your grasp.

The mental pictures you take with you – the initial mental experiences (after death) caused by your mental projections acquired in the physical body – do dissipate as the nature of the spirit takes its course. Then you get a rest from the mental gymnastics that ran your life and caused your suffering.

When nature takes over, the mental body becomes so at one with the universal mind yet it retains its individuality. It experiences real joy to such an extent that you feel there is nothing else on the other side but just you. And it is so pleasurable.

There is no such thing as loneliness or dissatisfaction in the subtle body. And, being attuned to the universal mind, you have a panoramic view, *in a subtle sense*, of all there is.

Some accounts about the immediate happenings after death depict that you go through a tunnel and a light comes to meet you. That is not strictly true. What you see is your own light that is within you, your own spiritual light, which you, after discarding the physical body, and just having the finer mind left, can recognise. You come face to face with your subtle body, which is not separate from you but is a greater you.

The dissipating remnants of the mind's images, because of losing consciousness when dying, which most of us do, could very temporarily feel that a tunnel is journeyed through. All images are just projections whether they are a tunnel or a person or anything else.

If you can achieve a fair degree of refinement you will experience a beautiful ecstasy, indescribable in words, transferring from the embodied conscious mind to the (body-free) subtle state in total consciousness, without mental images affecting you. This is known as dying consciously.

If you do not achieve such a refined state while on Earth you will still feel a wonderful sense of freedom, having shed the encumbrance of this physical frame. You move away from a grosser environment into a much more fine environment, a more subtle environment, when the conscious mind is deadened and no suffering lingers at all.

Self-Evaluation

When all the projections of the mind are sublimated, after first having a glimpse of the life you have lived, you start evaluating.

The evaluation is not a rational, analytical thinking process as we know it. It is natural and is very subtle and will always be totally one hundred percent accurate, being so close to the spiritual self. When I say the evaluation is subtle I mean it is a natural sense that takes over and not a sense that is reacting to any sensory input. There is no reaction or emotion involved. Your higher, pure self is predominating. You recognise your subtle self and it is totally accepted.

You evaluate not only this past lifetime but the entire existence of the individual soul that forms the subtle body. This becomes possible because, as you progress deeper into the subtle state, you don't hang on to the (three-dimensional) idea that evolution is a time-based concept.

The evaluation that takes place is based on the principle of evolution because, just as the physical body dies, the subtle body too will have to die at some stage when everything is cleansed from it.

The subtle body has greater strength than the physical body and it lasts many, many millions of years. The physical body has lasted for millions of years in different forms; right from the atom to the plant, to the animal, to the human, but is not continuous. The subtle body is continuous.

The subtle body lasts until it becomes free of samskaras, free from all the impressions that are clouding it. For although it is close to the spiritual light, and more of the spiritual light filters through, it does not filter through in its totality because the subtle body is affected by the various lifetime experiences.

The subtle body, being more open to the pure spirit, evaluates that it has to clean off all the dirt from itself and it never resists the cleansing method needed.

What is the best possible way forward? What is the best possible planet to go to now for a particular lesson that I have to learn? Should I come back to this planet or to another? What sort of form should I take? What would be the best path for me that would be most compatible for this entity? Which would be the best vehicles for this entity to take birth through?

All these evaluations are made by you. There is no father sitting up on a high chair, with books and an assistant, saying "Dearest John, on this date you did this and on this date you did that and this is how you will answer for it." You answer to yourself.

This is not in contradiction to any theology. This is in compliance with theology. Many of the things that are said in the religions are expressed symbolically but we have to understand the basis of the symbolism; the figurative meaning rather than just the literal value or just reading the words. We've got to read into, around, above, below and sideways of what is being taught. Then we can understand better what theology is trying to tell us.

In the individual personal judgment that occurs the great thing is that even the most dishonest or bad person, while living in the physical body, becomes the most honest person in his or her judging.

Each individual judges themselves accurately because there is a true feeling of joy and the greater joy is present to such a degree that the joy wants to proceed to an even greater joy.

Therefore there are no mistakes. It's like an inbuilt spiritual inducement. So, conditions for the next lifetime will be perfect for learning what has to take place in order to progress individual evolution to a higher spiritual plane.

Lessons cannot be learned in the subtle state. In that subtle state you remain static. You just function within yourself and within the boundaries of evaluation. There is no evolution, no moving forwards or backwards, in the subtle state. For any entity to progress it needs all three aspects of the individual self – physical, mental and spiritual. That is why our physical bodies are necessary.

That is why theology would say 'Your body is the temple of God.' Therefore this body is just as important as the subtle body. It is through the physical body that actions are performed. It is through the physical body that the subtle body finds a vehicle to experience or re-experience its own impressions.

So, do not under-estimate the value of the little 5 per cent mind we use while we are here. It is just as important as the dormant 95 per cent. But we can evolve faster and more joyfully if the 95 per cent dormancy is awakened while we are here. And, in awakening the 95 per cent dormant part while we are here, we doubly benefit ourselves on the other side because we have already started experiencing the reality of ourselves. Becoming familiar with it, we purify our mind and rise to higher dimensions in our rest state between lives.

It should now be evident that by doing meditation and spiritual practices you can help yourself in the afterlife as well as improve your lot while you are here. As the Bible puts it, you are 'storing up treasures in (your) heaven'.

Heaven isn't actually a place. You do not actually go anywhere in the subtle body. In truth everything takes up the same space – if you can call it that. Everything is here and now. All that happens is that the subtle you takes over, in the non-physical realm.

Where To Now; What Next?

As I have said, the journey is still a long journey for the subtle layers of the mind – the subtle body. Your samskaric bundle (of impressions) will choose which vehicle it is to be born through. We don't choose our children. Our children choose us.

In our subtle form, we choose our parents when we find the right genetic combination – the right level of evolution most compatible to the lessons we have to learn. This is why one person is born in happiness and another in unhappiness. This is governed by karma.

Karma forms an integral part of the subtle body. Karma exists in the subtle body in an impression form. Karma, which is action, transfers or transforms itself into the impressions (which we call samskaras). So, by thought, we produce action and by action we revert back into thought. It works in a circle and goes around and around – the subtle body going on, birth after birth, learning all the lessons it has to learn.

To help appreciate this, you could imagine that your subtle body is the director of your evolutionary story. In looking at the print it can sense that part of the text, even a single letter or a full stop, has faults, and the only way to perfect the adjustment needed is to apply a magnifying glass to the letters to see every little detail. The drawn out time and feeling of separation in the three dimensional sphere is the effect of looking through the microscope.

The adjustments cannot be made in the subtle body state; therefore your rebirth is the perfect magnification needed to potentially achieve the tidying up needed.

Now, in this mode, learning does not mean acquiring knowledge. It means shedding impressions. It means unlearning. It also means becoming non-attached, in the physical body – not by reading about it but by *doing* it.

Our subtle body is cluttered and what we call learning is actually cleaning up, unlearning, until it attains that state of purity. And when it attains that state of purity where all the unlearning has been done, when all the impressions are resolved, the sheath of the subtle body becomes totally transparent.

Then it merges into the superconscious mind. Then the subtle body disintegrates by merging back into the one-ness, just as the physical body has disintegrated at the end of a lifetime.

Impressions Are Thought Forms

No energy can ever be destroyed. Samskaras are thought forms and thought forms are energy. Energy just changes form. In this regard, the impressions you discard will be picked up by a soul evolving at a lower level just as you did when you took them on.

It is beneficial to remember this. You attach yourself to thought forms or detach yourself from them. You do not create them. This is not difficult to understand. Your individualness is not real – it is all in the mind – so how can it create anything?

I will not go into detail here but simply mention how, for instance, art of any kind is not created by the producer of it. It is all picked up by the subtle mind. Every thought, every idea, every composition that has ever been produced, or ever will be, is here and now. It is all a case of picking up on another piece of evolution you have not picked up on before.

The point here is a very important one. Thought is energy and your thought process is governed by your samskaras. And, thought is deed as far as your evolution is concerned. So, if you think negatively you will attract more negativity to you.

Therefore if you are a negative person you would be well advised to do everything in your power to dispense with your negative attitude. This is a practical matter and you do it by sheer determination.

You decide when you are going to change. Nothing outside you does that for you. Meditation and subtle energy practices may help to bring you to the stage where you want to change but you make the decision.

If you accentuate negativity here on Earth you will accentuate negativity more powerfully in the subtle body. Therefore you will give yourself suffering in the next lifetime until you break the circle of being negative.

Your life here is for the purpose of smoothing out your evolution. So, if you catch yourself feeling negative try to dispense with the negativity as soon as you possibly can – no matter what the situation or how much something might be hurting or upsetting you. Positivity is the single key to a better life here and a smoother life in the future. Negativity heaps bad karma on you.

Negativity is not in the flow of nature. You can only break the circle of negativity yourself. There is nobody in the beyond to say, "Oh you poor person, you have suffered, let me put that all aside for you."

If you think positively, which everyone is capable of doing, you will attract more and more positivity to you. As I have already stated, nothing is destroyed. Everything is energy, changing form continuously. There is positivity floating around you and there is negativity floating around you. You can have as much of either as you choose. Yes, if you are negative you are choosing negativity. Even though a negative person may not think this is a choice, negativity is simply a rejection of positivity, and vice versa.

So, from the conscious mind you clean up more and more of the sub-conscious mind. Eventually you get so clarified, so integrated, that mergence with the one pure consciousness takes place.

The amazing thing is that you can take millions of lifetimes or you can do it here and now. Just get yourself beyond the body, the mind, the sub-conscious mind, the superconscious mind and you can, here and now, merge into the highest consciousness. It can be done. Then you can say, "I and my father are one." This is another allegorical term, which suited the simpler minds of people thousands of years ago.

Most of us, though, allow our egos to master us for many, many lifetimes. We continue in this vein until some spark lights in us when we realise that embodied life holds no short-term or long-term permanent solutions and is only a testing ground, so we start wanting to change things.

Re-Birth
The average (Earth) time for a soul to be in the state in-between lives is about 30 years. Time does not mean the same, as it does to us, in the subtle body. The drawn out time experience in the physical body is necessary for creating the opportunity for the actions, changes and understanding we need to take on.

In the subtle body the individual soul is not really time conscious and it searches incessantly for the circumstances in which to be born. Each soul can sense what it will experience in its next childhood by being born of a couple who are about to conceive. Because of the make up of one or both of the conceivers and the future (known) outcome of the relationship between them, conditions of the soul's upbringing will be perfect for the rebirth in terms of tests needed.

Souls are flowing through such couplings all the time. There are countless numbers of them almost warring to attach themselves to the birth that will ensue from the coupling. This effort is not fighting as such but a continuous work-like struggle.

The soul does everything by feeling vibrations rather than thinking. The soul attaches itself to a male sperm, which fights to fertilise the egg. Each soul tries again and again until it is successful. Each life is willingly taken on as an opportunity – a precious gift.

There are no accidents about the circumstances of your birth. You pressed yourself into the opportunity, which is what every lifetime is, no matter what circumstances accompany it.

Do treat this life as a precious gift and an opportunity to realise your evolutionary status – and do something about it. That's what life is. You'll waste it all if you get caught up in too much trivia or the idea that temporary pleasures are the ultimate answer to the search for fulfillment.

Of course you should have lots of fun and pleasure. "Life without fun is an unbuttered bun," is one of Gururaj's often quoted sayings and is a great reminder to be light and positive. But do try also to come to terms with the bigger picture while you go along because that's what really matters to you.

The exceptions to the average time of rebirth are the highly evolved or the lowly evolved souls. These are a minority.

A highly evolved individual does not need many more lives. Their periods of peace, between lives, are extensive and will include rising to higher planes.

Becoming a highly evolved soul is not reserved for a few holy personalities. This happens to all individuals. You, whoever you are now, and whatever you have done in the past, will become a highly evolved individual and eventually merge into oneness. This is an unquestionable truth.

A lowly evolved soul will need a much longer period of reflection than the average, and it can find itself stuck for a long time between lives, in reflection and introspection, in a low plane beyond this one. This would probably include someone who has been responsible for causing a lot of suffering. These souls have a difficult task finding a suitable rebirth.

Religions might refer to this drawn out task of reflection and re-selection as hell. But there is no fire and brimstone or eternal torture going on anywhere in the beyond and neither is there judgment in other spheres by any other soul. Every soul seeks out the perfect circumstances for a rebirth in which to learn the lessons needed.

So, every person will pay back, as it were, during these time-imagined lifetimes in the physical bodies. Each individual balances themselves with suffering in the conscious mind and each suffering is an opportunity to resolve samskaras.

Therefore, if you encounter people who experience much suffering on Earth, be sure that the recipients are doing themselves a great service of learning and balancing. Do not judge them but be positive. You might even lend a helping hand sometimes. That could be positive for you karmically, if you have no underlying ego purpose for doing a good deed.

What I mean here is that spontaneously helping somebody in need is usually the result of a happy and open vibration in you, towards the world at large. Whereas, do-gooding, as a continuous specific activity, is often a cover up by someone attempting to hide away from what needs attending to deep inside them.

For the person who is suffering badly, their shortest route to overcoming their suffering is to accept that distress is an irrevocable, self-imposed self responsibility and to become positive in attitude. I will explore next the facts about paying off karmic debt.

You can be sure that before you came here this time around you predetermined the perfect circumstances in which you needed to be born. Nothing happens by accident.

The time you spend on Earth is more or less pre-determined too. In this regard a person who dies at a young age either does not need any further experience of being embodied, or they cannot gain further learning in this lifetime.

Children who die at or close to birth often need just the vague idea of being embodied, so as to complete their cycle of rebirth in relation to three-dimensional existence, before they move on to a higher plane. They feel the vibrations that are just right to complete their balance. This can also apply to someone who is mentally retarded.

If you are either reading these facts for the first time or refreshing your memory of them, then the time is right for you to be doing so. You bring yourself to do things by free will and by divine will. Divine will means the higher consciousness part of you that is moving you on by natural evolution.

You pre-planned the major turning points in your life while in your subtle-body state. Then you directed yourself between these points while in the body using your conditioned mind, but you are also assisted by varying input from your subtle mind according to your mood and your perception. This is your free will.

Yes, the unfolding of your life will be such that the major points of change are inevitable – predetermined. What happens in the years in between the major changes is entirely up to you. Your free will is both your power and your responsibility.

The more positive you are in moving on from the bad experiences you encounter, the more progress you will make. Free will cannot alter the major turning points in life but free will involves your attitude and this is what makes all the difference to your future.

No doubt a large chunk of underprivileged society would state, from this earthly-life viewpoint, they would prefer to have been born in different circumstances. This could also apply in privileged society where individuals can also sometimes suffer horrific childhood experiences.

But, in the state beyond, your bundle of impressions ALWAYS provides itself with the most ideal circumstances for progress. All the faults and disadvantages that accompany the individual's birth and upbringing are included. There are no mistakes. You cannot get away from Karma.

I am often asked if I think we belong to group families in this life and in the higher planes. I would answer this by saying that in this life we are frequently encountering souls who have the perfect vibration for us to align with, in order to test our ability to confront and to move on. Therefore our lessons are sometimes learned alongside souls who may have been relatives or close associates in past lives.

I do not go along with the idea of eternal group souls. We can move on from other souls whenever we wish. We will certainly always find further encounters with souls whose vibrations are perfect for testing us – giving us the opportunity to grow.

I do accept the concept of group karma where, for instance, a whole group of people suffer at the same time in one incident. Those individuals and their close ones who suffer as a result would all need the experience that befalls them. However the large number of people involved would not necessarily be connected to each other in their lives or learning patterns.

In summary, there is absolutely no alternative to your return journey to Earth, or a similar planet, to play out another role of experiences. There is no bargaining with any other entity on this score. Evolution happens whether you like it or not. And there is no such thing as *like it or not* in the state beyond. Evolution just takes place, in total precision.

3

Burning the Seeds of Karma

Removing
Self-Imposed Burdens

What is Karma?
The word Karma means action. We often refer to the *law* of karma when something strikes us and we can't think why we should deserve suffering. We muse that it's retribution for something we might have done, possibly unknowingly.

In the sense that every action demands an equal and opposite reaction, this general use of the word karma is correct. Every action in the universe has a balancing reaction, albeit the reaction is an equivalent in energy exchange, rather than needing to be a like-for-like repayment.

So the law of karma means cause and effect. It also means law of retribution and it also means law of balance.

It is useful to acknowledge that karma does not apply to mankind alone. It applies to every mineral, plant and animal. It applies to the planet, the solar system and the universe. For example, our universe must implode one day to complete the balance which it continuously undergoes. It cannot go on expanding outwards forever.

Although the wholeness that we really are is almost imperceptible, that wholeness is still there in every particle. The magnetism of the one pure consciousness is so great that it will never stop pulling us back to its purity.

This magnetic pull is not a conscious act by a (separate) oneness of existence. We are the oneness. Everything is the oneness. Therefore we are doing this magnetic pull ourselves. Nobody can ever stop doing this. And that is why we create our own karma.

Karma has arisen in each of us because our ego has interpreted, *within its confined limits*, what it accepts as actual and non-actual and what it accepts as true and false, good and bad, etc. And, we accentuate karma because we fail to live our life as a multi-dimensional consciousness. We live it as a few decades of experience, thinking that solid matter is everything and fearing when it will end.

We misconstrue our whole life foundation and mistakenly focus on the ego-induced erroneous conception that human beings are *actual*. This misconception is referred to as the cunningness of the mind. The mind tries to establish some sort of permanency in the unreal. This is the basis of all negative karma.

There is also good karma. Karma, being a balancing act, can over balance in both directions. So, you can build karmic credits too.

Should we just accept that karma sorts everything out and that evolution takes place whether we try to work at it or not? You can do that if you want millions more lifetimes of suffering because of inadvertently building further karmic debt.

Is there anything you can do to negate all that suffering ahead, to ensure happier times ahead? Yes, there are certain shortcuts that can turn your evolution around, stopping you from going further and further into karmic debt, wiping out your karmic retribution at speed – any speed you want to go at.

The Shortcut to Calm Waters
There are seven ways to resolve Karma.

First, *accept* what you really are and *acknowledge* that you are the result of your past actions, whether they are in this life or past lives. This is most easily achieved if you can get your head around the idea that you are the whole of pure consciousness and that each fragment-consciousness, which individuals are, must evolve due to the nature of consciousness.

Secondly, take on the *responsibility* for your past. By taking total responsibility for your current position in your evolution you immediately stop the out-of-control karmic train in its tracks and turn it around. You cannot progress substantially until you cease looking outside yourself to apportion blame for what befalls you. Action and reaction take place over innumerable lifetimes and you are responsible for it all.

Thirdly, you can invoke the *law of grace* by affirming to yourself that the energy of the universe will come to your aid as soon as you call on it. This is a remarkable tool to assist the self-improvement aspirant along the way. Although this is similar to prayer, the process recognises that one must deserve help in accordance with self-effort.

The law of grace can provide immeasurable assistance to you, in that for every step you take towards positive self-direction, subtle energy is attracted to you in at least tenfold equivalent to your own effort. These figures are hypothetical but the principle is fact.

Fourthly, karma can be counterbalanced by positive deeds and actions. As a simplistic example, if you become a doctor and save many lives, you could pay off the samskaric guilt you carry for having taken life in a previous incarnation.

There are innumerable other examples which do not necessarily work on a deed-for-deed or a thought-for-thought basis but the overall balance works out precisely. Becoming a goody-goody is not the aim here. The answer, for correct action, is to go along with whatever establishes an awareness in you of your Real Self.

By becoming provisioned with thoughts of wholeness (of existence), as opposed to the redundant perspective of *me and mine*, you will not go far wrong in starting to clean up your karmic slate.

Fifthly, the prepotent tactic for wiping out bad karma is to evoke a positive attitude. If you stop blaming anyone other than yourself for what befalls you, and take full responsibility for your life and everything about it, your whole evolution takes a major turning point for the better. You can do this here and now, in this very moment.

Sixth, you can assist a more real perception of reality by, for example, taking on some of the attunement remedies referred to in the final chapters of this book.

Finally, you can undertake stilling techniques such as meditation and other subtle energy practices. These will be more effective if personally prescribed on the basis of your present evolutionary status, your origin as an individual entity and your range of potential in this lifetime. Such practices will help you literally dissolve some of your karmic build-up by helping you release your conditioning, to some extent or another, provided that they are coupled with a *wholeness* perspective.

By means of these positive actions and attitudes you can fast-track to the position where you become the controller of your own destiny. Moreover, your previously held conviction that you are a little being of importance, limited to a few decades of life, melts away to reveal a feeling of greater self-strength.

Inexhaustible power comes into your domain, on earth, when you shoulder the responsibility for your evolution and cease to fear the end of this minuscule, restricted experience.

Karma and Reincarnation are in Relativity

Reincarnation is inextricably linked with karma.

When we talk of both karma and reincarnation we should remember that we are talking of limited reality, which applies in all the lower dimensions. Our surroundings are real to us but they are the result of narrowly limited consciousness.

One day we will rise beyond all this to see its futility. That day could come very soon after adopting a more real perspective of whole existence.

Gururaj asked his students to always bear in mind that these lower dimensions are all, in effect, a dream. Therefore reincarnation is a dream and karma is a dream too. He said this in order to assist, in the greatest measure possible, a truer perspective of our individual existence. Our viewpoint matters so much in bringing about our own balance.

So reincarnation, as well as karma, also functions in relativity.

In the absolute state of consciousness there is no reincarnation. It depends from what angle we view the theory, or the hypothesis rather, of reincarnation. If we look at it from a relative, rather than absolute, point of view then we could infer that there is reincarnation.

Atoms and cells came into being through the gigantic explosion known as the big bang and were propelled through time and space. As we know, time and space are also subject to relativity – and relativity in turn creates time and space. Furthermore, for time and space to be in existence there has to be a cause. The cause was the explosion which we refer to as creation.

In the evolution of the universe, the primal cells cross linked and developed into what we know as evolution in a higher state – that of the human being. Everything went through various processes and changes.

Cells have the ability to replicate themselves and when trillions of these cells are released simultaneously in an explosion, and each multiplies and interacts with other cells, the combinations produce other matter. (Like hydrogen is one thing and oxygen is a different thing, but the combination of hydrogen and oxygen makes a third thing called water). This chain reaction is known as *cause and effect.*

All these various combinations take place because of the propulsion created by the first explosion and it is the propulsion that we call evolution. We are propelled by this force to evolve. But in the process of evolution various transformations have to take place and these transformations are the things we call incarnation.

Each combination of cells evolves too, pushed on by the propulsion and, as I have said previously, each has a consciousness – a link between its present status and its origin.

So, for example, mineral (consciousness) evolves to plant, plant to animal and animal to man. That is as far as we have got on earth in the current *round.* This process takes millions of years and in the process all these various transformations include countless reincarnations. In other words every transformation is an incarnation. You come again in a different form.

You can deny the theory of reincarnation if you choose to do so because (sensibly and logically) you could insist that it has not yet been proven scientifically. But there are so many things that infer to its validity. Why is one person born in happy circumstances, why another in unhappy circumstances? The (divine) energy that is there (which we call God) is equable, is fair, and is just. How could it be fair to one and unfair to another? That is not possible. No neutral force could do that.

Reincarnation has to work hand in hand *with the law of karma*. They are part and parcel of each other that we ourselves have formulated when gaining consciousness that evolved into a discriminating consciousness. At first, in the primal stages, we were just pushed by this force of propulsion. After that, the combinations and multiplications caused hybrids of matter and hybrids of consciousness.

In the process of evolution when *advanced* consciousness dawned – when the power of discrimination dawned – from that moment karma started assuming its own values. These values are governed by our own selves, our own discriminatory factors.

In relativity what has happened is that from silence an explosion has occurred and we are caught up in the propulsion, which resulted from that explosion.

That is why we say we are here by divine will. What we term divine will is propulsion and we are part and parcel of that propulsion until the momentum of the propulsion wears off and we return to silence. So we come from silence and return to silence. We come from God and return to God, as the saying goes.

Within the boundaries of relativity, we say that divinity permeates all relativity because the propulsion we are caught up in is energised by *that* energy. Therefore divinity exists in every smallest grain of sand and in every single atom in this vast vista of the universe.

But when we look at it from the absolute point of view, or

from the point of view of that original silence, even our simple minds can logically interpret that silence does not require reincarnation.

In the relative, reincarnation is necessary. In the absolute, all the relativity and the reincarnation theories, and the theories of evolution and the theories of karma become just a dream. To use an analogy, the depth, the silence, of the ocean is not aware, in its silence, of the turbulence of the waves on the surface, even though the turbulence exists in its wholeness.

It is not important whether you believe in reincarnation or you don't. Each of us is equipped with such a wonderful mechanism – that in spite of all the outward surface turbulence each can dive deep within ourselves and experience that silence; the primal silence of our being of millions and trillions of years ago. The outer expression could not have been there without the inner expression. Each person can confirm this fact by experience.

When a human being experiences that original silence within, all the problems of life cease to exist. The experience of that silence brings forth the knowledge that the saying 'Peace, be still, and know that I am,' is a definitude.

Then too comes the understanding, with total and willing acceptance, of the expression, 'For all this too must come to pass.' By experiencing pure silence you acquire *knowledge*, by recollection, that all this turbulence is transitory. Anything that changes is non-eternal.

Once somebody has tasted eternity they are not going to worry about this non-eternity, these superficial little problems.

As you untie the samskaric knots, karma will ease. You will come to know that you are not who you have been thinking you are. You are not Jane or Jack or Jemima or John (or whatever name is ascribed to you). You are the Real Self of you, which is pure consciousness, and not the individual energy entanglement that has patterned your thinking and actions for so long.

In starting to ease your karmic load by means of the attitude of self-responsibility, I would remind you again that, as well as being the debtor of your past, you are also acknowledging your full accountability for what you do from now on.

If you are wealthy and healthy and happy you have deserved it. (The wealth factor is a matter of personal choice which I will discuss under Prosperity Consciousness). If you have no troubles, you have evolved yourself into such a position.

If you have a sublime life now, remember to be watchful not to abuse your position because you can easily slip back down the karmic ladder. Hold in mind that thought is deed, where your evolution is concerned. We do slip back from time to time in the process of evolutionary progress if our thinking goes unguarded.

If you are unhappy, deprived, depressed or unfortunate, you are reaping your own karma which you have sewed yourself. Fortunately, because of the laws of nature, you can turn that position around with lightning speed. By way of meditational and unconditioning practices, more and more subtle power is felt and your own vibrations can be heightened to such an extent that a lot of your karma passes away. It is dissolved unnoticeably and without suffering.

There are no mistakes – none whatever – in the circumstances in which you find yourself. You have provided these circumstances in absolute precision. There is no getting away from this. Karmic balance is like a magnet based upon subtle energy vibrations.

Our personal attitude towards our karma is of fundamental importance. Whatever you do, don't let your karmic burden depress you. We are all here, trapped in our mind turmoil but with the opportunity to release ourselves from suffering.

You should not focus on the suffering. Life is for enjoyment as well as self-accountability. You are not going to get far by being a parched, colourless character who takes the attitude, "Woe is me and my responsibility for my evolution". You need to enjoy yourself.

"Life, love and laughter," was Gururaj's most formidable motto. You can have endless fun drawing to yourself more or less anything you wish for by being open, jolly, outgoing and light-hearted. These are all positive energy dissipations. You will not assist self-power and self-liberation by oppressing yourself.

Do We Need Angels?

There is no ultimate *big boss* to look up to who could possibly change your fate or bestow favours or forgiveness on you. The patternings of your mind, which you can change but from which you cannot escape, are the ultimate deciding factor regarding the direction you will take from here.

But you *can* get extra assistance when needed. You provide the help yourself, as I will explain, when you adjust and align yourself appropriately vis-à-vis your evolution.

But are there really intermediaries in this or other spheres and what help can you rely on from them?

This is the question of intercession. The question is, "Are spiritual mediators existent or necessary to help you in this life or in the afterlife?"

The Quest for Help

The majority of us, at some time or another, become confused, doubting, sad or in need of help in some way that cannot be satisfied by contact with our fellow humans. Therefore we might ask for *help from above*.

The idea of angels and guardian angels is necessarily a supposition because all realms are forms of mind.

So, the essence of what I am saying here is that within the framework of limited reality, within relativity, there *are* forces in the cosmos that are of a like nature to each of us. Like nature means that there are individual forces of a higher vibrational substance. Like us, they have limited existences.

It is by means of heightening our vibrational status that we will attune to those higher vibrations – call them angels, guardian angels or whatever. We can draw those higher vibrations to us to help us. But if we can experience the highest state of consciousness while in this human form, it means we have traversed other existences beyond us. It would be a direct line to Divinity – to the highest (absolute) vibration possible.

First, what is an angel?

Angels have not transcended the boundaries of relativity. It is said in some scriptures there are seven lower forms of existence, and there are seven forms of higher existence in the universe. These existences are all relative and mankind is roughly in the middle. They are all the same really, but the difference is in degrees of consciousness related to evolutionary experience.

The lower forms of existence have an instinctive way of life that is not guided by intellectual capacity, and it is only when we reach the stage of mankind that consciousness comes into focus and the intellect starts working.

As well as mankind being reborn on this planet to learn certain lessons necessary to evolve, there are also other forms of existence where the individual still needs to learn. But the learning is in a different dimension – or different degree of awareness.

There are many evolved beings who have become masters of the three dimensions we know of. But even for the advanced soul's progress there has to be learning in the fourth dimension, the fifth dimension, sixth, and so on until the individual goes beyond individuality, reaching the stage of absolute-ness where he or she merges away in the totality of all existence.

When we talk of the various levels of existences, we are talking in a linear fashion controlled by time and space and causality. But the higher levels of existence are also subjected to some rules of time, space and causality.

Remember that different dimensions have been created by mankind for a need, a necessity. And that necessity is always for the sake of evolution. When we use the term *dimensions* we mean there are subtler qualities of the individual that are exercised.

Mankind can perceive, through different and greater dimensions, a state where everything is of such a subtle matter, and that subtle matter is far more interpenetrating than the matter we know of here.

To use an analogy, we have a block of wood over there, and we have another block of wood over here, and we experience, because of our limitations in three dimensions, that the two blocks are separate. But in the fourth dimension, also ruled by relativity, one does not experience the separation. And that is where verbal and physical communication becomes unnecessary.

In the higher realms the grosser senses that we have here – hearing, touching, seeing, smelling, tasting – become unnecessary, because we have now gone beyond the need of the senses. So in another dimension the communication can be automatic rather than having to be transferred from one being to another by some sort of carrier mechanism.

On Earth, the average person can experience subtle energy by means of extra sensory perception (ESP), which most of us have a taste of at some time or another. This is the *knowing* when something is about to happen. It's a non-verbal communication where the thought is just picked up. This level of consciousness is experience that cannot be intellectualised.

A human being is capable of experiencing all the other dimensions, but does not hold on to the experience because of the (necessity of) the ego. Living in this embodied form, these glimpses can only be made permanent if the mind is stilled enough.

The angelic kingdom is one of those experienceable dimensions. In all these various levels of existence we operate upon different levels of the same mind. As I have explained, the mind is as vast as the universe. The degree is one of grossness or subtleness.

Do not confuse this with any form of mediumship. This is often confused, so I want to emphasise the point. Beings in any angelic kingdom do not have the time or the inclination to have any contact with earthlings. Their mind does not descend to our level. As I have already stated, mediums use solely their *own* mind, albeit in some instances it is their higher mind (and in some cases it can be a disturbed mind).

At the three-dimensional level, we live with the conscious

mind. An animal lives within the flow, within the propulsion of evolution, devoid of conscious consciousness. Psychologists would term this the collective instinct. These are definitions.

Mankind has advanced a bit more than the animals, where the grosser level of the conscious mind is used. So it stands to reason that there could be other entities living in higher dimensions that could exist in a stage that is more subtle than the conscious mind that man uses.

In the angelic kingdom, the subtler level of the mind is used. Using the subtler level of the mind, one experiences greater joy. It is not the (eventual) supreme joy but in the angelic state one experiences a greater joy.

Who reaches that stage? The person who has lived these lifetimes and has become a master of the conscious mind does. And mastery of the conscious mind can very consciously be brought about by right thinking and right action.

In summary, you *become* angelic, i.e. you raise your vibrational level by overcoming the grosser mind levels. The human being does not contact individual angels. Nor do angels contact humans.

Are There Such Things as Guardian Angels?

In effect, as far as our mind is concerned, yes, there are guardian angels. Where do they come from? Again, man/woman creates everything in his/her mind. No-one else creates it. Therefore, once again, each person, if they have a guardian angel, creates it for themselves.

The range of the human mind is as vast as the universe. But where else in that vastness of the universe is there a place for the guardian angel to stay? Everything is now and here. So the abode of that guardian angel *must* be within the framework of your mind.

There is a finer energy, a subtler level, within your mind known as the Sattvic level of the mind, which reflects the spiritual self in its greatest glory. So when the conscious mind is calmed, sometimes it is said that a little voice whispers within. That little voice is not from outside. That little voice is from inside you but at a subtler, deeper, purer level. And that is your guardian angel.

Because of its purity and because of its strength everything at a subtler level is far more powerful. It is always there at your beck and call to guard you. If you are open enough to that force, if you refine the conscious level of the mind, you draw to it the finer, purer, subtler, more powerful vibrations which come to the conscious level and you feel guided.

What the whole matter of angels really means is that you are drawing from deep inside. Everything is within you. When it comes to decision making or discrimination, you will spontaneously make the right decision if you have allowed the depths of yourself to come into play.

To provide you with as much clarity as possible and to further elucidate on frequently asked questions, on the often misinterpreted subject of angels/guardian angels, here is a word for word *extract from Gururaj's response to a question on this subject (in 1977):

> "Angel is a funny word. Why not call it a guardian 'angle'? It is the angle from which things have to be viewed. That is, the practical angle. There are theories, mythological theories perhaps, where there are angels floating around all over the universe. This is true because your mind is as vast as the universe and they are floating around in your mind. They can be made into a tangible form by your mind and through your mind, because it is only one mind – the universal mind – and it is we that have individualised it, individuated it.
>
> "So if a person says they have heard the chorus of a hundred thousand voices that could be true. I have experienced these things myself. But where did it come from? It did not come from outside of me. It came from within me, where the mind has been taken to a level to tune itself with the music of the spheres; celestial music. Man is capable of all that. And if you really want to see the angel, you can see it too. You can materialise what you regard to be your guardian angel by yourself, by the power of your mind.

"And if your mind is an illusory mind – which it is – then your guardian angel is also illusory. But within the concept of the illusion, it is a reality. It is a reality within the framework and the boundaries and the concept of Maya. Maya means our attachment to our perceptions. It is real to us. Everything is as real or unreal as you make it. You can look at a teacher or you can look at your beloved as someone Divine, goodly, godly. Or else, you can look at the teacher or your beloved as just another piece of flesh. The conception is yours. Everything exists. Anything which the mind is capable of conceiving or thinking is existent and created by the mind. The mind creates the existence of its every thought. For nothing comes from nothing.

"On this subject, I have given the example of a poet. A poet does not create a poem. He / she could never do it. But he can attune his mind. And neither a painter nor a composer is a creator either. He can attune his mind, to a certain level, where in the cosmos, all these poems, all these thoughts, all this music, all the concepts and colours in painting are floating around. And if you are properly attuned at the right moment, like your receiving station, your little radio, you gather those thoughts. And gathering those truths in your poems, you portray the truths through the mind. And the purer the thought, the greater the truth that comes through in your poetry is dependent upon how clear your mind is. This means that your mind acts as a filter.

"So the guardian angels are there, which are created by the mind, and by the mind we can give them a reality by which they can be heard and seen. But remember, the mind is creating that reality. The mind is manifesting it."

The complete Gururaj UK satsang reference CD 'Answers To Your Life' contains hundreds of transcripts of Gururaj's talks together with summaries of each talk and a subject index reference table

Can the Personal God Help You?

You do not need to be mystical or pious to discover that God is an impersonal energy.

Science has now reached the stage of the proof that we have been awaiting for millennia. Dr Stephen Hawking, the world's best known evolution scientist of the day, has quoted in recent times (circa 2000 A.D.) that the recent confirmation of multi-dimensional existences will probably lead us to the conclusion that God, the original almighty energy, is impersonal. This means that the source energy and its manifestation is natural and does not purposely create.

Such contemporary celebrities agree that everything in existence from the lowest to the highest dimensions is combined energy.

This bears out most of what I have already said about existence, which may add encouragement to readers who are encountering these ideas for the first time. It also bears out what thousands of mystics have said, down the ages, long before these scientific detections were made.

Nonetheless, these facts by themselves don't bring total satisfaction to the enquiring mind. We need methodology that can provide comfort, hope and greater potential to the individual.

Most people need a personal god or an ideal in their mind because a human mind can easily relate to an image of another human, whether living or not, whereas some vague idea of energy can't be seen or imagined. That's reasonable, isn't it? It's not viable to ask someone to describe the taste of sugar if they've never put sugar in their mouth.

Furthermore, revered spiritual personalities, known as *gods on earth* – because they had *all* knowledge – are very easy to relate to because they are thought of as pure. Each is a personality who can be looked up to for guidance and help. There is nothing stupid about this. We base our beliefs, about the unknown, on trust. This spiritual trust has become known as faith.

Faith is naturally engendered in our minds when we are

drawn to someone who we feel knows what they are talking about. Not least, devotion to a personality can bring about effective results. It is your sincerity that counts in this respect and not which path you have chosen or believe in. All knowledge is within us but we need a focal point to hone in on.

Each great master is valid. After they die they are venerated and imagined as God. This is valid too.

What has happened here is that the body of the master who has passed on decomposes like any other body but the spirit of the master passes to the highest realm possible. Having said this, the only difference between these people and ordinary people is that they have realised that they are not a person in this realm or in the highest of realms but that they are what I have referred to as the eternal Is-ness, which is beyond even the highest realm.

So, is there any point in directing faith, which is belief rather than evidence, to what we may consider to be a spiritual master?

The answer to this question is yes.

As I have explained, angels come about by utilising subtle degrees of the mind. Angels are of a like vibration to an individual who would call upon them for assistance. They might be used in situations of either need or of guidance or simply wishing for more love and peace on the planet. The assistance that comes to you is not an activity by any other being. It is an activated subtle energy vibration.

Now, the true spiritual master represents the highest vibration. He/she has gone beyond all realms of individualness or duality.

Can you access the highest vibration of the true spiritual master – the so called personal god – whether that master is alive or deceased? In other words, is a direct line between you and divinity, avoiding all the intermediaries, useable?

The answer to this question is also YES. Everything is one. There is no time or distance between you and the personal god vibration or between you and the impersonal god vibration. It is a matter of personal acceptance and attunement for each of us to discover that this is true.

The highest vibration is here and now, in the superconscious level of your mind, and that very (subtle) level of your mind is available to you without interruption.

Consequently, why would anybody call on the vibration of an angel rather than the highest vibration in existence?

I have confirmed for myself, as have millions of others, that the angel – the subtle energy vibration close to your own level of vibration – is a limited source.

If you are seeking substantial change, the highest vibration is your greatest support. Additionally, the highest vibration has an infinite range; therefore it can provide assistance with the smallest of problems too.

Calling upon (or aligning yourself with) the highest possible vibration has great effect. For me, there is no point in doing anything else. Whether I want a parking space or financial or practical help, a cure for a disease (for myself or someone else) or spiritual guidance, I use what is sometimes termed Shakti, which means the most refined energy source.

In effect, the highest vibrational level of the mind compares to what some call the Jesus consciousness or the Buddha consciousness, etc. You, the ordinary individual, have the highest consciousness too, albeit veiled from your immediate recall.

So, unless your religion precludes it, there is no reason why you should not use your chosen deity as a trigger to bring your most refined, ultimately powerful, subtle energy into your daily life to help you in a practical sense and to self-direct your path (and your desires) in the most appropriate way.

I have seen what appears at first encounter to be virtual miracles in the lives of people who have drawn from the Shakti level of subtle energy, either by simply imagining an image of their deity or by using a vague awareness of Shakti (without using any image).

For simple examples I would cite
    a) Getting a new job or dispelling financial difficulty;
    b) Providing basic necessities, time after time;

c) Finding items, that have been lost for weeks, within 10 seconds to 10 minutes;

d) Receiving contact from a distant friend by simply commanding it.

The more extreme examples I can verify are

e) Recovery from a near death situation (by several people *sending* Shakti to that person using a distance healing technique);

f) Winning a high court battle against very long odds;

g) *Instantly* walking several steps after having not walked one step for 14 years, followed by, within a few months of the first steps, dancing!

h) Many cases of much enhanced wealth, status, etc.

The examples I have encountered myself are so numerable that I have forgotten many of them. I have quoted a mere handful above, from the experiences of people I have known. Based on my experience so far, I would say there is no difference, in terms of results, between using an image of your selected deity and by summoning the highest unseen energy by any other way you imagine it.

Gururaj used to say that you need an external guru until your inner guru is awakened – emphasizing that in actuality they are both one and the same thing.

What becomes apparent is that the more you practice aligning yourself with Shakti, (or whatever name you want to call the highest vibration of subtle energy), the more competent you become at using it without necessarily imagining someone or something else channelling energy on your behalf.

Shakti can't be defined so I will use an analogy. When the sun shines, it shines equally on the meanest person and the most highly evolved one. They both benefit from the heat of the sun. Even if we are not highly evolved we still receive the benefit, the heat, the light, the nourishment from the sun. So it is not necessary for a person to be highly evolved to be able to use Shakti. Everyone can use it.

A term for the use of our personal deity as a channel is *Gurushakti*. This fine vibration also draws on the highest subtle energy in relativity. Guru just means from *darkness to light* whether or not the word is used to represent a person.

Angels are of a subtler realm but, like us, not of the ultimately refined vibration which is the ultimate goal. Therefore, unless you want to dabble with energies of a less than pure state, which will not guarantee to smooth out your evolution, and could harm your progress, there is no point in trying to align yourself with any vibration other than Shakti.

4

Unconditioning –

Take Control and Exploit Your In-built Resource

You are now aware of what existence actually is, how your mind misinterprets it, and how it is possible to utilise subtle energy to enhance your potential. You will be further advantaged by knowing how to untwist your samskaric bundle of impressions so that you don't block your access to the ever present potent subtle energy, which can be used in so many practical ways.

If you have read books that spell out how to use the law of attraction – which I recommend you do – you will doubtless be excited that, by applying the law, you can change your life almost instantly.

The law of attraction is an indisputable, natural phenomenon which most people fail to use because they either disbelieve it or don't give it a fair try. This means the majority of us fail to grasp what is within our reach all our life, while *wishing* we could have had a better deal.

In my experience, the majority of people who attempt to gain health, wealth and relationship advantages using the law of attraction fall short of their target, in many cases miserably. The reason for this is that to use this law effectively you need to be at least a little bit *integrated*. By this I mean that subtle energy needs to have permeated your mind to such an extent that you have identified the ego's hold over you and started to silence it.

Books on the law of attraction wisely advise that it's not effective just to think of what you want. You have to feel that you are already in the position you want to be, because thought is energy and the universe responds to what is in your mind.

However, your mind is underscored by the samskaric patterning of your past, which affects the way you think. So, however much you soak yourself in the thought that, for instance, you are a millionaire, you are always operating from the foundation of the patterning that invisibly controls the mind and the subconscious, silently insisting that limitations are good for you.

The effect of visualisation will be severely restricted while your mind-conditioning is opposing, unwittingly, what the universe is trying to provide for you.

You need to become a blank sheet – at least for short periods – on which you can rewrite a new blueprint of yourself, otherwise the old pattern and the new pattern will jumble up together, preventing clarity, and you will not progress to the new position you desire.

This is where unconditioning comes in.

Unconditioning won't take anything away from you – it will put you in a position to be able to add all sorts of benefits to your life, including commanding whatever you want by means of subtle control.

Unconditioning allows you to align yourself with the universal mind, so that you can use the law of attraction effectively.

Unconditioning is a combination of quietening the mind and re-mapping it. I often call it *mind bathing* because that's all it is. You gently bathe your mind to rid it of the build-up of dirt. This enables you to avail yourself of the endless store of better-life goodies that awaits once the dirt is washed away.

Unconditioning could be likened to cleaning out a rusty old washing machine so that it can clean clothes perfectly again. While the rust prevails the clothes always come out less than clean. The mind, covered in samskaras, is much the same.

The mind can't be totally effective in using the law of attraction while, in its make-up, there is an inbuilt resistance to solving the problems.

Unconditioning will work hand in glove with the truths

depicted in the previous chapters, to help you unfold sufficiently to discover and be able to use your inner potential*.

Based on what you have already learned, start to hold in mind the principle of the wholeness of you until the little-ness of you is seen for what it is – irrelevant. You will become more and more effective at doing this as unconditioning progresses.

What Is Your Goal?

Why did you decide to read this book? Almost without exception, the underlying reason will be a search for greater happiness or satisfaction during this lifetime. This may or may not include a desire for greater knowledge of the purpose of life or how you can improve your afterlife and future lives, or it may be solely to improve this current lifetime.

Greater happiness is available to every person who will just turn on the tap in accordance with the laws of nature rather than restrict themselves by sticking solely to what went into the mind during childhood.

Most peoples' upbringing didn't include even basic tuition about why we're here, what you are responsible for in your evolution or how you can adjust your journey to become free of the suffering caused by your problems. Thus the limitations of the self-strangulating conscious mind were exacerbated because you learned trivia, via memory tests. Fact, whether general or specific worldly knowledge, are of no use in the matter of self discovery, which is the primary route to controlling your destiny.

Now, if your primary concern is to pad out your present lifetime with greater comfort and a reduction in suffering or problems in general, you are in the right shop, reading books like this one. But I advise you *not* to skip straight to the section on procurement or you will miss out on some fundamentals you need to know in order to be able to magnetise whatever you desire.

In order to shortcut to life improvement *quickly*, during your tour of self-betterment stores, be sure to pick up the goods marked 'nature zone'. The merchandise that appears, to your senses (because of your previous conditioning), to be marked 'comfort zone' is often a mirage, just like the illusion of water in a desert.

The goods marked 'nature zone' will allow you to flow with ease to wherever you want to go. I'll explain further as we go along. I'm speaking metaphorically here, of course, so don't go thumbing through the pages literally looking for these labels.

Whether your desire is for self-power, improved relationships, wealth, health, or for self knowledge, everyone who becomes fully integrated with their universal (subtle) mind is joyful, content, mostly unaffected by problems and can attract to themselves what they desire. Moreover, almost everything is changeable in a very short time indeed.

The majority who attempt change drag out the time span of the change because samskaric patterning is very convincing! But, in actuality, the universe does not have size or time constraints, so there is nothing outside you that can prevent the change you desire happening more or less instantly.

All that is required to commence mastering the antics of your cunning mind is a total commitment to a new viewpoint as to where you stand in the order of things. In this task you will be assisted by taking on simple meditative techniques I will describe, along with day-to-day-living practices, to help re-attune the conscious mind. I sometimes refer to the day-to-day practices as attunement tools.

Attunement tools can hardly be called techniques. They are more a way of thinking. But they definitely help to sublimate the dance taking place between the ego and the intellect. Their use can minimise restrictive barriers formed by the mind.

Attunement does not interfere with any chosen lifestyle. Attunement ideas and practices can be taken on as you wish, if you wish. They will support the positive effect of the Balance and Alignment techniques (I shall first describe). Balance and Alignment techniques also support the principles of attunement, so the two work together – inseparable in terms of being the tools that will enable you to eliminate suffering and enjoy life to the full.

Recommended Balance and Alignment Techniques

"It is through these meditational practices that we can activate the subtlety, the subtle powers of the mind, and dive deeper within ourselves so that the subtle powers can be brought out into the grosser form of life and thereby make the grosser form of life more dynamic, more vital, more powerful, more harmonious – and that would be called living instead of existing." – Gururaj

First, a basic balancing technique is personalised meditation: This takes up a slot of time in self-seclusion – say six or seven 20 minute slots per week on average (or up to double this amount if you can afford the time). The effect is firstly relaxation and then, more importantly, dealing with thoughts so that ineffective, wasted thought spirals loosen their grip. Consequently the time-wasting and *suffering* elements of the thought process subside and the mind is able to convert into an efficient, servile tool.

A personal technique can be individually prescribed based on a person's evolutionary position (picked up via their vibrations) and their potential in this lifetime, as well as on the source of subtle energy. Generic mantras can also be useful.

The second technique is focal gazing, often called Tratak, part of which is visualisation: A candle flame is a most effective tool but, with experience, any small object can be used.

This helps with
- a) concentrating more effectively,
- b) becoming less fragmented,
- c) accessing the inner subtle energy resource with greater ease and
- d) improving the effectiveness of personalised meditation.

Moreover, this focusing technique helps to increase the production of melatonin, a renowned good health abettor in the human body.

Thirdly, subtle energy deep breathing and subtle energy permeation. This practise allows you to align yourself with the vibration of the refined efficacious energy of all dimensions. This can also be used when in need of instant calming or support.

Fourthly, chakric energy helical movement, sometimes referred to as swirling: Based on moving subtle energy through the chakric system. This works on removing personal energy entanglement blockages within both the subtle body and the three-dimensional body systems, which are superimposed upon each other. (Acupuncture and other subtle energy purifying techniques are similar in effect). Consequently there are healing benefits too.

Certain counts, time frames and other instructions apply, for the above mentioned techniques to have maximum effectiveness. Therefore, personal guidance is required. Also, there are advanced practices for those who wish to deepen their evolutionary experience.

The majority of these practices do not take up significant separate slots of time but are structured within the conscious mind during daily activity once continuous practice becomes more or less automatic. They are mostly silent but deeply profound. They become effortless after a little practice.

At first glance the above list may seem complicated. But it isn't complicated at all. Each technique is very simple indeed; each is learned in turn and very quickly fitted into daily life, more or less as habit. Apart from the few specific 20 minute slots each week (which are very enjoyable because they are relaxing and regenerating) most of these practices are done with less effort and less time than it takes to fix a slice of toast.

The mechanics of the whole package of techniques – the reason they work – are that they change the way a person reacts to thought. The upshot of this is that an inner balancing takes place. Thereby the process of nature is re-harnessed within the individual, which is totally harmonious for mind and body.

Harmony within us is our nature. It is our birthright.

Disharmony causes disease, a shortfall in our desires, shortened life and unhappiness. Virtually every disease has psychosomatic origins. And, all personal conflict in relationships is some sort of disharmony between those involved caused by samskaric (reactionary) patterning.

Balance and alignment techniques are practical tools for regeneration and reacquiring the art of living in a mode of maximum joy.

Wherever appropriate the techniques should be combined with the following unconditioning maxims – and any further effective ones you can find elsewhere. The combination is fundamental for personal unfoldment.

In short, samskaras cause off-balance. The use of techniques and unconditioning reverses this imbalance.

The Principles of Attunement

The Three Portals – enter them for a deluge of wonderment and wisdom

The mind has to justify its own existence. The masterful ego directs you to target an imagined set of desires or circumstances. This energy wasting hyper-activity builds web-like barriers to the flow of nature.

This does not mean you shouldn't have personal goals. Having focussed goals is good for your wellbeing. It's the continuous 'idea images' that are the energy wasters.

By means of effective meditation and other balance and alignment techniques, we can minimise the mind's wasted energy component and increase true focus. A change in perspective creeps up, more or less unnoticed, on the ego.

From time to time the ego may snarl and bite back, which is noticed in what we call personal growth. You can soon recognise this when it occurs. It shows in your resistance to something via a connection to one of the three subjects mentioned below.

To overcome this resistance, make sure you are genuinely thinking, as much as possible, about the wholeness of yourself – the bigger picture of whole existence as well as the limited life you live on Earth.

The ego lives in the lonely condition of the *little I* concept of life. Remember, this life is an imaginary condition so it is not real. But the ego battles away in a sometimes very convincing manner.

Nevertheless, subtle energy predominance will win the inner battles! Feel the power of your subtle energy and you will rise above any struggles.

You need to be aware of the 'whys' and the 'hows' of the three vitally important portals to understanding, so that you put yourself in a position of potential success.

The portals may have been like solid walls to you in the past but they are really the access to your new life. The portals are Acceptance, Non-Attachment and Change. If ever you become in any way confused about changing your life for the better or attracting to you what you need or want, I would advise that you remind yourself of one or more of these three elements that can either control your life or free you unimaginably. Referring back to them continuously can bring clarity into often muddied waters.

Acceptance – the single step to everything you could wish for

"Be free to accept and therein lies your freedom" – Gururaj

When you come to recognise that your ego is only a reflector for higher consciousness, and has no reality of its own whatsoever, your concept of life alters. If you constantly remind yourself of this factor you will loosen the stranglehold you have allowed the ego to exert on you thus far.

It is simply a matter of *acceptance*. You are not Jack or Jane or whatever name you use. This is the principle to accept. You are the whole of universal consciousness, not a miniscule part of it.

I am not asking you to 'accept' what I say in an undoubting

manner. I don't encourage blind belief. I encourage *discovery*.

Doubt is positive. Doubt improves your self reliance, which eases your route to improvement. But you have to open your mind to new possibilities if you are going to give yourself the option of discovery.

To commence, be open minded to the fact that you are not restricted to being a three-dimensional object but that you have many more dimensions within your consciousness. This might be new thinking to you but it has a sound foundation, since it is the result of scientific investigation.

Later, when you have experienced for yourself the power of your subtle-mind energy, you will be satisfied that you know your higher consciousness and its power, which belittles anything you achieve by using your senses, your memory, your intellect or your ego. (Revert to the Mind-Works diagram in chapter 2 if you need clarity here).

At the stage of *knowingness* your acceptance of these basic facts will be real and it will be complete. Knowledge is the only position from which you can be sure. Until then, doubt everything and explore the possibilities.

Don't worry about killing your ego. No part of your mind is going to disappear! By introducing the idea that the ego is not really in charge, you start to *refine the ego.* You stretch the ego, rather than annihilate it. The ego then becomes useable rather than dominant and delusory.

Therefore, do not aspire to get rid of the ego. This is impossible while you are embodied. Your objective should be to *master* the ego. You stretch it so it can be seen through. In this way the ego's activity can be observed, like a play. By doing this, the ego's (borrowed) power to inject needle-like pain is taken away.

By opening up your mind to all possibilities you start to stretch the ego, and you soon realise you are a much greater being than this mortal, temporary blip. You start to see through the facade. You control the ego. The ego's cunning game is up!

When you *insist* that the ego is not in charge, much more universal force is allowed to flow through you. The ego in turn starts to lose the power you previously let it have and which provided all your sufferings by limiting your vision of reality.

Now, the intellect is what stands between you and reality. The intellect builds barriers. One of the greatest barriers it builds is a self-protective haze which you, subconsciously, think is preventing your childhood hang-ups from upsetting your life. This gives you your traits, most of which are barriers to the Self.

But when you come to true acceptance, your problems all vanish. Compare this to psychiatry. Have you ever known of a person who underwent psychoanalysis and all their problems vanished? No.

In essence, therefore, true *acceptance* of what you are is the only aspect you need to add to your personality to solve the whole of your life. You probably won't evolve to true acceptance overnight because you have quite a bit of mind-stuff to uncondition. But it can be achieved in this lifetime.

When you are around a person who has developed true acceptance you will witness a personality that is unaffected by anything in this world. This is not a brain-washed person but a person who has come to terms with their multi-dimensional wholeness through certain knowledge.

Attachment – to nothing but an idea

"We live in a dream world. And all things that are imaginary, creating imagined needs, are illusions. And all illusions are fleeting; never, ever lasting. What we want is something that is forever lasting and never changing, and that comes about by diminishing the needs, the desires, and becoming non-attached."

Gururaj

A fundamental and critical ingredient for self discovery and self power is non-attachment.

I use the analogy that attachment is the glue that holds in place the cunning web spun by the ego and the intellect, which provides an effective but temporary barrier to perceiving your actuality. The purpose of glue is to attach.

Furthermore, attachment, while acting as the adhesive that holds the ego web in place, also provides an opaque screen, by means of added illusory mind-stuff that prevents you from expanding your consciousness.

Typical of the confusion aspirants sometimes have about attachment is the story about one of my students who asked if their attachment to chocolate or meat was likely to stand in the way of personal unfoldment. Although this can be somewhat amusing, it depicts clearly an area where mistakes are commonly made.

Attachment is not about desires or fads or day to day habits. I am talking here about the prime attachment, which is the only one you need work on – your attachment to the *little I*.

Focusing on the temporary, boxed-in *little I* causes you to project that all other faculties are *outside* you. But in truth – in actuality – everything is within. Everything is accessible and controllable from within.

You are not going to lose anything by becoming non-attached. Non-attachment to the idea of an important little you is, again, only a matter of perspective. Non-attachment is not throwing yourself off a cliff!

Non-attachment is an important goal in controlling your own destiny. It can be reached in an instant, once you decide non-attachment is what you want.

Becoming non-attached is not becoming detached. Detachment is removing yourself from your surroundings in a reclusive manner, whether this is in either a physical or a mental mode. To achieve non-attachment, you must be involved with life to the full but not be reliant on anything outside you, especially the end result of your actions.

I am often asked how it is possible to become non-attached to our near and dear ones, especially our children. The answer here is to be attached in a non-attached way. What exactly does this mean? It means that we have to live this life focused on its reality – live every moment of it fully but have your mind open to your *actuality* all the time.

Naturally, most of us want the comforts provided by companionship and our relationship with others. But your need to hang on to people and other things stems from a need for love from outside yourself.

In truth, all love is from within. A needy love derives from insecurity. Pure love has no needs and is given and received without attachment to any end result. This may be easy to apply to feelings for our children but not so easily with love for partners, because love for partners mostly assumes conditions.

Having said this, many parents also have conditioned love (or needy love) for their children, continually seeking their attention or their presence. Again, this is caused by attachment to the little self, causing the need for outside padding, the ego once more being in control.

Both acceptance and non-attachment can be unfolded in you to some extent as can all the unconditioning methodology I will now discuss.

All of this will help you gently advance your perspective without detracting from the full enjoyment of life that your children and other relationships provide for you.

Everybody I have ever met who undertakes the subtle energy practices together with unconditioning methodology has said that their relationships improve.

The reason we improve all aspects of our life via non-attachment is that it accords with the continuous flow of nature. Nature has to flow, it cannot stop. Attachment is an attempt to resist nature.

A soul that is exceedingly attached will delay its rebirth because there is a resistance to what nature is determining. All resistance to the flow of natural evolution causes misery or suffering of some kind.

Change – The best-kept-secret personal tool for providing newness, opportunity and endless enthusiasm

> *"Lord, grant me the serenity*
> *To accept the things I cannot change,*
> *The courage to change the things I can*
> *And the wisdom to know the difference."*
> – Serenity Prayer

Our third portal is change. Everything changes. You cannot alter this fact. Nature is change. Change is nature. But the energy we use up in trying to prevent change is so enormous that it takes years off our lives. Much of the time we are not even conscious that we are trying to stand still.

We resist change because of fear of the unknown and because we think our individual lives are the most important thing in the universe – and that death is a tragedy.

Because we are fearful we try to hang on to things as they are while, at the same time, we are struggling to change things for the better.

One concept is fighting the other, isn't it?

We fear letting go of anything or everything to which we have become attached. This is an inbuilt patterning which is an underlying reflection of our fear of death – the giving up of our earthly body.

So, why don't we look at change positively? Change is inevitable. Change is in the flow of nature. Resisting change is painful. Flowing with it isn't painful at all.

I often refer to the story of about a Chinese woman of 121 years of age who, when interviewed about her secret of longevity, said, after a long, pensive pause, "I welcome change".

This little story speaks volumes for itself. Welcoming change melts barriers, reduces wasted energy, reduces stress, improves health and extends life. All this prevails because we flow better with our evolution, a consequence of which is to immensely increase our power to reach our goals.

Changes are necessary – and, if you think about it, desirable – to bring about improvements to our life because we need to alter what is going on today in order to get something more satisfying than we already have.

It's all in accordance with nature, isn't it? Change happens to every aspect of the universe, every nanosecond.

There is a simple solution to overcoming our resistance to change. In our Earthly consciousness, we relate to 'things' in the three dimensional sphere. We continuously project, as if using an imaginary cinema screen, that we can extend our power base and improve our happiness and comfort zones if we hang on to everything we have and (possibly) add something to the pile already acquired. We also project that we might weaken or become less happy if we give up what we already have.

The answer is to *eject* rather than *project*. If you take on the idea of ejecting thoughts and circumstances that are holding you back – after thoroughly examining your life and your patternings – you will start to feel enormous cleansing.

When you eject things from your mind, not only do you free yourself but you coincidentally take on a greater degree of self responsibility which results in an increase in self power.

To eject does not mean to jettison everything and everybody in your life. Ejecting may at some time mean moving on from a person close to you, or a deep-seated set of circumstances, if you are fighting an oppressive or constrictive exigency prevailing at any time. But the idea generally, if you want to use ejection to change your life for the better, is not to 'chuck out'. The idea is simply to remove obstacles from your path.

The more you attune yourself the more you will emphasise shifting obstacles so they become less irksome, rather than trying to add paraphernalia to existing conditions.

Once again, the overriding factor to assist you and assure you of greater stability is that you become used to the idea that you are not your ego. You are the whole (multi-dimensional) you and not just your ego which is very limited.

The ego is a trap. It has no foundation so it is continuously trying to create images of a little stand-alone three-dimensional you. All discomforts and suffering stem from this delusion. By getting used to the *whole* you, all the empowerment you need to stop your mind wasting vital energy is at hand. You can command the little mind to become a practical, utilitarian mechanism.

When you *invite* change you resolve within yourself that life as it is today cannot ever stay the same for very long. You accept what life is. You cease to hang on too much to things that will inevitably disappear. When you achieve this you will be able to float through this life like a leaf on the wind, putting the maximum into it and thereby getting the maximum out of it. You will be what is termed, by Gururaj, "*In the world but not of the world*".

Despite its fight for predominance, the ego will eventually lose the battle because we are by nature all moving towards expanded consciousness and nothing can stop this process. It's the rate of the process that is the choice of each individual.

The *idea* of discomfort is what most of us battle against. But this fight is unnecessary.

Each of us lives in a comfort zone, accepting in our psyche what we think will keep us from harm. The alternative zone to live in is (what I term) nature zone.

Nature zone is full of change. Our ego tells us not to go there. But nature zone is where our whole self is, so by seeking comfort instead of nature we miss out on 90 per cent of our self-power.

How do we overcome this dilemma? It's really very simple – give nature zone a try. By trying out nature zone as opposed to comfort zone you are going to experience a new joy of life that will have you dizzy with wonderment. You will wonder why you ever restricted yourself to comfort zone. You will also immediately realize too that comfort zone is where all your problems are, whereas you'd previously thought that it was nature zone that was the threat to your happiness.

This transformation happens because it is *your nature* to experience change. When you live in comfort zones you are fighting nature and getting nowhere. You are trying to hang on to a particular set of circumstances. This is impossible. Change has to take place.

When you welcome change you flow with nature so smoothly that you are uplifted and the shackles of life fall away. With that, you cease to insist that one set of conditions or another individual (in your life) is what makes you happy. Then your relationships actually improve because you have moved beyond what your ego had you restricted to. Then you dance through life rather than shuffle.

When you dance through life in this way you are in step with yourself and you have no doubt that it is YOU who makes you happy, whatever circumstances prevail from time to time.

In summary, let's re-emphasise the following point. In achieving maximum self-power, which is our birthright, we do not have to dispense with our goals or our loved ones. It is *change of perspective* that achieves personal improvement, and not necessarily a complete change of life path.

Nonetheless, I personally advise removing obstacles that attempt to cause any oppression or restriction of liberty. I don't think it is a good idea either to suffer at someone else's hand or keep close to those in whose company you feel a heavy vibration, thinking that it might be good for your soul or helpful to the aggressor. A willingness to suffer is not the way out of bad karma. It's positive attitude and flowing with your Real Self that turns the tables.

"We have come to this Earth, we have chosen this incarnation. In the modifications the soul has to go through, one needs strength to bear the consequences of changes... A change has to be there sooner or later and one gains inner strength, through meditation, to bear these changes more easily. Yes, one has to bear the cross – you have no choice – but it has its rewards. This is a great truth." – Gururaj

5

Attunement Tools and Triggers

You will be pleased to know, if you don't already, that there is only the faintest whisper of difference between the great achiever and the non achiever. This also applies between the sad and the happy, the fulfilled and unfulfilled and between those who can alter their destiny by a mere thought and those who cannot. The faintest whisper of difference is that little something we have referred to many times already – perspective.

What I am saying is that virtually anything can be achieved given that the aspirant's perspective is aligned with acquiring and achieving the goal in mind.

For instance, the rich get rich because they have no resistance to riches. But most people do have a resistance to becoming wealthy, often because they (subconsciously) think it is either not possible for them or not good for them. Such compelling thoughts come from outside influences and not from the purity within.

The same applies to all aspects of life, be it material acquisition, love, blissfulness, fulfilment, overcoming problems, controlling your destiny …. Ad infinitum.

It's no good trying to use the (very natural) law of attracting whatever you want to yourself, while your inner make-up is pulling in the opposite direction.

For most people, their adult life and achievements are based on their psyche which is constructed in childhood. This is where the patterns, which form both resistance and limited perspective, are established. But you can change immeasurably by using the techniques and practices I've mentioned, *coupled with a determination* to uncondition your old ways of thinking.

The following tools and triggers can help you to re-align your perspective of life and therefore the way you deal with it.

We have already discussed in chapters 1 and 2, the workings of the mind and how our existence operates. Once you understand these fundamentals you will be able to use unconditioning to grow away from a small world viewpoint, thinking you are a suffering, mortal being who is answerable to an authority separate from you. This will introduce you to and help you take on a more expansive consciousness which confirms that nothing is greater than you; that you are the wholeness of all existence and you can assume its power and flow of love whenever you wish.

At this stage, I would advise you to make sure you have read and fully understand the content of the first three chapters herein and become reasonably content with it.

The Essential Precursor: Uncovering Yourself

To unfold your potential you first need to take a cool and sincere, decisive, non-deceptive look at yourself. You need to uncover what your samskaras have determined by way of thought patterning. This is otherwise known as facing yourself.

I knew very little about facing myself until I got closely involved with Gururaj, in my mid-thirties.

Like most aspirants of self-betterment, I had read about the concept of being true to oneself with regard to personal faults and frailties. However it wasn't until Gururaj said, "If you truly face yourself, you will not like what you see," that the full force of this component of personal unfoldment really hit me.

To face yourself is the mechanism that helps you to uncover personal traits, the existence of which you are often not aware. You are not aware of them because you don't want to face them.

A very close self-examination of your personality is needed. But it can be a bit like a detective story – not being able to find what you're looking for!

To understand and accept your patterning, and help remove fear that might emerge from truly facing yourself, you can try to imagine standing outside yourself and examining a person you are not involved with.

As a further aid in this task, you may like to imagine that you are another being altogether, who is observing a person just like you. Appreciate carefully the person in front of you without judgement.

To repeat, facing yourself is uncovering yourself. There are things within your personality that you don't want to face. This applies to everyone.

First, always take account of the fact that every human being is imperfect and has countless faults. By appreciating this you will more readily search for your own weaknesses without putting yourself down for being what you are – the product of all your previous experiences bearing down on you.

Every person has faults and no one person is better than the other just because their experiences have taken them on different routes. All our paths are different. Look at these facts, and at your personality, as dispassionately as possible.

Secondly, recognise that you are an escapist. Without exception, everyone is an escapist. This means that while grinding away at achieving your ideas of perfection you are pasting over the cracks that need repairing. Those cracks need to be fully and permanently cemented rather than loose-filled.

In most cases, individuals deny that the cracks exist. The escape act referred to here is your conscious mind trying to deny the existence of samskaras. Samskaras contain faults and impressions that support your ego, whose existence relies on the constant whirling around of your projections and impressions.

I personally spent more than a decade (of denial) getting to the point where I admitted to myself that my life from age nine had been a series of escape attempts due to the death of my mother at that time. What I now realise is that I could have come to that recognition in a few weeks, or even a few days if I had dropped my guard, so to speak, and allowed myself to feel my fears and weaknesses.

What most of us tend to do is to take on the amount of truth that the mind finds acceptable at any one moment in time, causing us to build more patterns on a foundation of part-truth. This results in an equal or greater illusion.

Conversely, we do have the ability to improve our lives permanently by referring back our reactions to our traits, our traits to the causes of our traits, and our patterning to our evolutionary status.

Everyone can do this. It is not difficult. However, sticking to the truth about yourself can become a toilsome task if you don't recognise your own inbuilt resistance.

The idea is to strip yourself bare, metaphorically, to reveal the unadulterated you. This pure unaffected you is there all the time. What is needed is to dump all the froth that your mind continuously stirs up. You need to get to the heart of you to understand why all the stirring is happening.

The wonderful thing about facing yourself is that it is a process of releasing yourself – from both the imprisonment of the mind and from the turmoil that the conditioned mind causes.

You can start by looking at your body and your body language and the things you do and the way you do them. You might need some help with this. Be brave and ask others to be absolutely truthful about how they see your traits, your habits, your bodily stance, etc.

Put your mind (and your reactions) aside and be prepared to hear a lot of comments you don't want to hear and with which you'll probably instantly disagree. Persist with the exercise, even though you may not like it at first. It can actually become fun.

Little or nothing can be done to change many congenital predispositions but they can still be observed as a temporary evolutionary need.

Concerning your traits, your mind will keep insisting that both the way you are and how you act are either wholly or approximately acceptable. This is because you live your patternings and you put up with them, despite the discomforts you suffer. Most of us thereby deny that the things that repeatedly go wrong in our lives are patterns. Typically, we blame others for what goes wrong.

Keep putting your mind aside. If you truly observe, rather

than be involved, *as if you were observing someone else*, you will start to see yourself as the person you have made up since you were a child. Eventually you will admit, "This is my shortcoming, this is my weakness, this is what I need to do. These are the conditionings I need to address."

The object of facing yourself is to get away from the idea that you are an important focal point in this universe. You could compare what you see when you observe yourself – a trait-infested humanoid – with, say, a misshapen or crumpled leaf, or something else that represents nature, which needs ironing out to get it back into shape.

Don't worry about throwing yourself away! Once again, you are not going to do that. This is only an observation exercise, albeit fairly detailed. You are simply going to unattach yourself from your surface mind. When you achieve this you will feel remarkably buoyant – and free. This whole exercise becomes easier when you are established in meditational practices and the like.

By frequently repeating the process of facing yourself, you are able to acknowledge, "I am nothing but these self-constructed patternings." Then the realness of you has dawned in your heart. You observe how the sense of the little 'I' is conjured up. You start to see beyond the sense of the ego.

I have known some people, and heard about many others, who overcame seemingly unconquerable diseases by honestly facing themselves and challenging their conditioning. These diseases include alcoholism, obesity, low self-worth and cancer.

Do not fret about putting yourself down in any way during the process of examination.

Realising that "I am nothing," is *not* saying, "I am nothing *compared to others*". Realising you are nothing is concurrent with realising that everyone else is nothing too. This will give you a lift rather than put you down because you realise that everyone is exactly the same – nobody is any greater than any other, despite some people's trappings, qualifications, (superficial) knowledge or whatever.

When considering mind traits it is not difficult – if you are serious about it – to identify how and why your mind operates as it does. You don't need to spend countless hours on a psychiatrist's couch if you are really open and honest with yourself.

This is not to say that psychoanalysis is not a good thing on occasions for unravelling a buried experience or two, in order that you can pinpoint the reason for a trait. But it is best, in my view, to move beyond those experiences rather than to keep reliving them. Focusing too long on the dirt does not clean it away.

One method you can use to relieve yourself of the effect of re-living past experiences is to *intensify*. This means allowing your-self, for a short time only, to revisit a hurtful experience intensely as a mental picture and to try to feel the emotion of it. This allows you to let something go, from your stored up mental impressions. Additionally, you show yourself the experience is definitely of the past, i.e. it does not now exist any longer. Thereby, you can de-cide that it need not affect you from now on.

It is best to do this just once. If you find yourself drawn back repeatedly to intensify one particular experience, then you would do better to seek professional help in order to clear up the continuing effect of it. Whichever, you will come to the conclusion that you decide everything. *You* decide when to move on from letting a past experience affect you.

Once you know where your traits and thinking patterns stemmed from, your experiences can be observed as a step in your personal history. Put every experience in perspective as a part of your whole evolution, acknowledging that any harsh backlash you received was to accentuate a lesson you need to learn.

You have billions of previous personal experiences but they are only a story and you have to move on. After intensifying any bitter experiences, in order to relive the experience and what it caused in you, 'burn the seeds' of that experience by imagining the redundant remains of an imaginary furnace to be stored away in your burnt seed box.

You can't take away or obliterate past experiences. To attempt to do so will erect further personal barriers. What you can do is look at them as having once been a growing seed which troubled you in the past. Thereafter you have fried them and popped them into your 'past experience' burnt seed box where they will have no affect whatsoever on your present or future.

Burnt seeds can no longer grow. You can look at the burnt seeds as the enrichment in the soil in which you now grow the flourishing plants of new life. You will be helped by accepting that you give yourself all the experiences of life in order to grow more joyous by means of self-challenge. And you will be further assisted by recognising that the experiences of this lifetime are but a few compared to the millions from your evolutionary past. This puts things in perspective regarding your experiencial *needs*.

What everybody discovers by self examination, as we have discussed, is that thought patterns are largely a product of childhood experiences. What many of us do, for instance, is to keep imagining the unfairness of childhood experiences – often subconsciously – trying endlessly to somehow make good past shortfalls. Whereas, we could alternatively take the more positive view of admitting that our personality, based on whole evolution, needed every single experience encountered.

As far as our thought processes are concerned, our parents should not be blamed for acting out their own traits – which we might suffer from or pick up on. We chose our parentage, based on our evolutionary needs. The major occurrences that happen to us and the major turning points in our life are set in stone, so to speak, before we arrive here.

Do not interpret facing yourself as a route to becoming some meek, subservient sponge. Recognising your true condition – that you are no thing – is not belittling. It's quite the reverse. What you are recognising is that your *mind* is nothing and that you, yourself are the eternal oneness – the ultimate power and that the 'little I' is insignificant. In this way you infiltrate unlimited strength into yourself.

With new strength you will be in a position to reject any negativity in yourself and in others, rather than accept it. This opens up a whole new world of positivity and a determination to be self-reliant.

Not least, facing yourself has an added benefit to those who have previously put up with another person's vexatiousness, disruptiveness or even cruelty. It will become clear that we have drawn such things to ourselves and we can change the circumstances whenever we make the decision to do so.

The Kick-Starter: Conscious Effort

Conscious effort should be considered as the process of initiating positive thought that leads to change or accomplishment.

To use an analogy, it's like the washing-up that gets more and more onerous every time we think about it, but, once the commitment is reached to start, the job just flows and is no longer mentally fatiguing.

In other words, there is no more effort needed to work towards solving a difficulty than to suffer from it. You are depleted of more energy by suffering than by solving. Moreover, as difficulties start to be eliminated, which they will be when thought and effort is correctly directed, the benefits of positive action start to flower immediately.

Here again we involve our free will. Each of us decides how to utilise our free will.

It is vitally important to recognise that free will cannot be jettisoned. Like it or not, our free will bestows upon us, and highlights, our self responsibility. We have no alternative but to *use* our free will.

When we accept this, we come face to face with the decision of whether to do something positive or something negative. Doing nothing, in attempting to solve difficulty, is negative. Doing nothing to solve inertia is negative. Doing nothing about your *dharma is negative, if you are aware of dharma, or circumspect at best. Thereby you restrict your evolutionary progress.

Dharma means using positive attributes in a positive manner. The literal translation of Dharma is 'duty'. This does not necessarily infer duty to others but more to oneself, by making the best of life using free will. If we consciously make effort to improve our own lives, positivity gathers pace for us and reflects on those around us. Conscious effort is the principal constituent of performing Dharma.

So, lethargy or complacency does not absolve us of the responsibility that our free will demands of us. Using your free will to decide to do something – *anything* – however small, is the key of positivity that is always waiting to be turned. It will lead you to a more joyous road ahead.

There is one additional mental attribute required for conscious effort and that is commitment. Commitment ensures that benefits continue. Without commitment, free will is wasted.

Evolutionary progress can be severely stilted or even reversed at the human stage unless you *consciously* progress it. Conscious effort is therefore vitally important.

Conscious (mental) effort directed towards acceptance of the universal self is something that each individual decides to apply whenever the time is right for them. Acceptance of your universal self allows your little I identity – your ego – to refine itself enough to commit to a totally self-reliant and self-accountable pose.

Remember in all this we are seeking balance, not extremes of experience. It is balance that brings about integration. Integrated people take part in the world in full measure, but they are not affected by emotional turmoil. That is why an integrated person has absolute power over their life and their destiny. They will experience the same knocks in life as everyone else but the effect doesn't last. They quickly move on.

We can all do with as many tools and triggers as possible to help us with conscious effort and commitment. I have the following extract by Goethe on my kitchen wall:

> "Until one is committed there is the chance to draw back; always ineffectiveness. Concerning all acts of initiative (and creation) there is one elementary truth, the ignorance of which kills countless ideas and splendid plans – that the moment one commits oneself then Providence moves too.
>
> All sorts of things occur to help one that would not otherwise have occurred. A whole stream of events issues from the decision, raising in one's favour all manner of unforeseen

incidents and meetings and material assistance which no man would have dreamed would have come his way.

Whatever you can do or dream you can, begin it! Boldness has genius, magic and power in it. – Begin it now."

Goethe

Inertia

"Arise, awake and stop not 'til the goal is reached."

– Swami Vivekananda

If you happen to be at a stage in your life where you are suffering from inertia, be sure you're not alone. You could be reading this book, which contains a lot of advice about positive action, in order to benefit yourself. At the same time you could be finding it extremely difficult to get the energy together to do something. This lethargic stance is caused by many external factors and can at times seem like an impossible negative spiral.

In this regard you might like to try the anti-inertia 'game' to help get you out of the pits. I made it up for some of my students but I've used it myself too. It seems to work quite well. It's called Moment One. (See Appendices at the end of this book.) There are lots of other therapies around if you need them.

The secret of the anti-inertia game is physical movement which interrupts the trap of lethargy. When you move your body you change perspective, because your senses alter. When the body becomes active, the mind eases because the analytical side subdues and the creative, more natural, side comes into play. You can do this as often as you like to dispel lethargy and promote positive thinking.

Every movement is also conscious effort – appropriate to what is needed at the time. The effort you put in need only be small, provided it is positive, but what eventually results from your commitment to it can be quite amazing. Conscious effort can be considered as putting in our 10 per cent in order to allow nature to do the other 90 per cent of effort. But without the little initial effort nothing will happen at all. This is a similar principle to the Goethe quotation above.

The principle of positive action produces everything. All man-made progress stems from a thought. We can help ourselves further by being choosy with thoughts, so as not to delay the positive effect of our kick-starting action.

Whenever possible, do not use the phrase "I *will* change", because that is an escape into further inaction. When you want to affirm change you should always carefully state, "I *am* changing …" This affirms that the process of change is now in progress.

Self Responsibility & Self Reliance

By accepting the law of karma (refer to chapter 3) you come to terms with the fact that you are responsible for all your actions. Karma literally means action. Action implies movement. Movement is motion, an energy interchange or exchange of some combination.

If you live your life based on the principle that someone else or something else is responsible for you, you may also allude to the idea that there is a being somewhere who can bestow forgiveness upon you. But this is simply not true.

Moreover, by refusing to accept complete self responsibility for your existence, you can easily become lethargic about changes that are needed. You would then have little interest in getting into action to sort out your own evolution. Consequently, you can slow down your evolutionary progress or become somewhat ineffectual in terms of either accomplishment or personal happiness.

When we live life on the basis of the law of karma, we accept that every action must have its corresponding reaction. This applies to the greater universe, to the planet and to each individual. And, to emphasise once more, as soon as we take on the view that we are totally responsible for our own evolution, we take a gigantic step towards greater self power and accomplishment.

Haven't you noticed how you can be let down when relying on someone else? It doesn't matter if it is an employer or a close friend or relative, you can never totally rely on others. When you rely on yourself, nobody can let you down. If things go wrong you can *always* do something about it. But it is you who has to bring in action. You *must* instigate action. When you act you are on the road to solving something. And, when action is continuous, you can solve anything and reach any goal.

The same applies to thought. Thought is a tangible energy. If you apply positive thought in any situation, you drive yourself to a positive outcome. If you apply positive thought continuously you become a positive person with a favourable life, with positivity coming back to you.

What you must take into account, in terms of self reliance, is that you have not always been positive in the past. Therefore you must reap what you have sewn, albeit you are not conscious of events in past lives.

In this respect we can be sure of one thing. There are no accidents. Down to the tiniest event, energy in its many forms is balancing itself out. And, as mentioned before, this applies particularly to thought because thought patterns are samskaric. This is vitally important to accept because thoughts are the basis of all activity.

In terms of self-reliance, what can we do about the past? Yes, we can simply put it away! This is where acceptance and change come to the fore. We cannot change the past, which has left us with some karma to dispel, so we must take courage and see through whatever befalls us in a positive manner.

Positive thought and positive action will dispel (bad) karma far quicker than lethargy or sorrowfulness. We should never think in a 'poor me' fashion. Self pity is negative output which attracts more negativity, according to the law of attraction.

The word 'bad' in the previous paragraph is parenthesised to highlight a commonly misused term in relation to karma. Actually, there is no such thing as bad karma. What happens is that we bind to ourselves samskaras, which means we carry forward energy patterns which we previously created by way of thought or deed. Samskaras are impressions that stick together in bundles.

Samskaras are resolved by resolve. In other words,

steadfastness and determination relieve us of negative traits. Every adversity has opportunity knitted into it.

We have to accept positively the circumstances in which we find ourselves. We are the cause of what life brings to us and we can *always* do something about it! Gururaj adored the stanza, "Two men behind prison bars; One saw mud, the other saw stars." Every pitfall provides an opportunity to strengthen our resolve.

I distinctly believe that when religions refer to 'sinners who repent', the origins of such phrases, rather than being moral judgements, lie in the fact that a person has turned away from negativity, self pity, reliance on others etc., and has motivated self responsibility, positive thinking, acceptance of the Self and the determination to move forward progressively.

The attitude we take towards life's predicaments and the circumstances in which we find ourselves is a personal choice and a significant free will factor. If you want to become more self-powerful and happier, it's not much good saying, "It's my karma," or "It's meant to be," about everything that goes wrong or turns out less than desirable.

Conversely you can say, "Here is a situation I needed to experience because of my samskaric patterning, and I declare my immediate action to change things for the better." This is the approach to take. Samskaras are *tendencies that are changeable*. They are not set in stone. Changing our samskaras is the same as altering our perspective.

It is immensely beneficial to acknowledge that we answer only to ourselves. This approach helps us keep focused on providing everything for ourselves including the changes needed, the consequence of which is to attract a greater flow of positive energy.

6

Further Adjusting Your Perspective

Thought Control

"Be careful with your thoughts, they are just as powerful as deeds... Whatever you emphasise, you are ruled by."

– Gururaj

No truer word has been spoken, with regard to accessing and utilising the potency of your subtle mind, than the above quotation. Because thought is energy, thought *is also* deed. Thought will either burden you with karma or relieve you of karma just as much as action can relieve or burden you.

Why is thought the same as deed? Thought is a dissipated energy. Dissipated energy cannot be eradicated, it can only be counterbalanced. Every bit of energy gets propelled onward.

Be even more careful with your thoughts when you reach a high degree of integration, because your thoughts will have gained so much more power. This care should come with ease, because your desires and judgements will have become refined.

Of prime importance is what you do with your thoughts while you are unfolding. I am not anxious about over emphasising this point because I want to impress upon you that here is a real opportunity to stop amassing 'bad' karma.

The last thing I want you to do is build up any guilt. Guilt is by far the largest karmic binder and most of it is unnecessary. Doing ordinary things that all humans do is nothing to be guilty about. Mistakes are a part of life's learning path and not a guilt dirt-bin to carry around with you.

A fact to accommodate here is that you are acquiring karma, which causes unbalance in you, all the time you refuse to flow with the nature of evolution. You can lessen the amount you accumulate from here on, reducing your self imposed suffering, if you cut out negative thoughts.

Accepting self-responsibility for your evolution – like it or not – is a positive action because it is controlled, positive thinking, which is a prime karma dissolver.

Whatever you feel guilty about, *forgive yourself* for past events. The past is over now. Once you commit to being totally positive, you can dispense with negative thoughts and experience a remarkable transformation. Truly feeling sorry is a great aid to moving on from the past.

The evolutionary laws of nature will ensure that we return to the consciousness of the Real Self. Everything we do to interrupt this natural flow is keeping us in the quagmire of unreality.

Thoughts can help you flow or can stop you flowing. Free will determines how we will use our thoughts. Accepting your evolutionary status and doing your dharma is getting back in the mainstream of evolutionary flow – where you belong.

Don't be too concerned about your desires. Having desires is perfectly natural and should never induce guilt. Your desires will change, anyway, as you become more integrated with the subtle side of yourself. Your desires in the most part aren't hurting anybody. Well, if you find any that can hurt others, do dispense with them.

You have to look after yourself in this life so you must do ordinary things, but it is your responsibility, as you will find when you assess yourself after you pass on, not to negatively affect others with either your own preferences or your attitude.

The worst thoughts that bind you are judgments, misappropriated criticisms and negativity of any kind.

It is not difficult to stop having negative thoughts if you continuously put in the effort to do so. You simply summon up positive thought to dispel negative thought. Light will always outshine darkness.

Your conscious mind can help you in various ways if you pay firm attention to it. Take the example of putting a sign on your kitchen wall that says, "Think enthusiastic – Be Enthusiastic." Such simple steps promote positivity in you and others.

One of my firm favourites is in my bathroom. It reads, "The Ten Most Powerful Two Lettered Words – 'If It Is To Be, It Is Up To Me'."

I will address positive thinking again under the subject heading of Contemplation.

Discrimination

"Discrimination is the jewel of wisdom"

– Shankara

Discrimination is an absolutely essential subject to explore in the area of thought control, as well as in the area of self discovery. It is by far the greatest sphere of mind activity in which we make mistakes about our evolutionary progress. We want to rid ourselves of mind-stuff that causes karma but the misuse of our ability to discriminate is possibly the topmost cause of our own suffering.

The general idea we have of being discriminative is to use judgement selectively.

In the matter of unconditioning the mind, a very different picture emerges.

The mind, because of its conditioning, instructs us to silently verbalise whether each idea or fact it encounters is right or wrong. Then we slip each piece of information into its appropriate slot with a label saying, "I think this is right". The result of this, down the ages, is that morality has taken over from purity.

In our society today we have to inject morals to defend against harm of people's bodies or their property. This is a fundamental administration for the good of all.

However, most authorities introduce very few rights and wrongs for our personal protection but many, many rights and wrongs (ideas) to get people to be subservient and respectful of, or even fearful of, authority. Why do you think governments all seem to accede to the idea of a supreme authority in the heavens? This very idea keeps the masses thinking that authority over them is correct.

Umpteen morals, therefore, seem to have taken the place of the laws of nature. We have become ego orientated instead of real-consciousness orientated. We have developed a sense of right and wrong that can often take us away from our Real Self. It's not our fault. We take on what we find as acceptable during our formative years.

In actuality, in pure consciousness, there is no right or wrong. Therefore, to climb out of the junk-mind spiral of self inflicted masochism, we should seriously look at the continuous judgements we make unwittingly, following on with assessing where we are being unnecessarily accepting of things that can be changed.

The difference between animals and humans is that humans have the power of discrimination. Humans have the power to rationalise. But mankind loses out because the power of discrimination is not used wisely. Each should make a conscious decision about what is natural and what has evolved via committee-orientated decree. All of us have this responsibility. You certainly need to use it if you are going to improve your lot; eliminate your suffering.

So, use your head. First decide what proper discrimination is and secondly discriminate in the way that your discriminative faculty was meant to be used. This will involve assessing what is real and what is unreal, which is true discrimination. You will be greatly assisted in this essential task by reminding yourself what is temporary and what is eternal.

All judgment and all suffering stems from the fact that the human mind is biased towards sensory input and therefore attaches more importance to the temporary than the eternal.

The process of discrimination, coupled with contemplation, awareness and letting go (see chapter 7), is a most useful pursuit you can undertake to disperse the veils of ignorance that prevent you from perceiving your true nature.

You can support self-monitoring of your discriminative faculty by constantly reviewing what happens by nature and what mankind has invented. To do this you may be helped, again, by imagining that you are some sort of extra-terrestrial being who is observing this world and who is not a part of it.

Being indiscriminate gets us wound up, gets the mind more and more clouded. Meditational practices and unconditioning help to refine that cloud. We change the cloud into other forms, where the light can penetrate. Whenever we feel stillness, our natural inner subtle energy comes more to the fore so that we can guide ourselves naturally, without analysis.

When you don't bother to discriminate, and you jog along constantly repeating your past actions, judgments and analysis based on the way you or the people around you take for granted, your discriminative faculty is not working any more. The nature of you is put farther into the background.

The upshot of being non-discriminative could easily be that instead of progression there is retrogression in your evolution.

To use an analogy regarding evolutionary progress, on a foot rule the mineral kingdom could be, say, three inches, the plant kingdom would be the next three inches, the animal kingdom from six to nine inches and the human kingdom the final three inches. It is not possible to slide back below the nine inch mark once you have entered the human realm, but you can slide from above eleven inches back to the nine inch mark.

The power of discrimination, (Viveka, as it is called in Sanskrit) is given to us for one purpose and one purpose only – to be able to discriminate between the changing and the unchanging, between the relative and the absolute. For the absolute is our real essence, which is changeless, while all the changes are the manifestation of that one changeless-ness.

For us all to live together on this small planet, rationality and moderation are required. However, rationality and moderation are not reliable on their own. Being rational and moderate might seem like standing in the centre of a see-saw, but each person, in this way, continues to judge because each person –

without the final ingredient of *discrimination* – is selective of thought, based on their conditioning.

True discrimination is not conditioned. It is unconditional. We utilise it by looking at both sides of every issue from a higher perspective.

By continuously looking at the *big picture* we use our discriminative faculty better because, by doing so, we reduce our tendency to analyse. We thereby help to keep our view and *our perspective* balanced. Accordingly we advance our vision of life as it is and not what Maya would have it to be. (Maya means attachment to our perspective).

When learning to be less analytical, we should once again hold in mind that the ego cannot be cast aside. The ego dominates our deliberated thoughts as well as our instant thoughts. Analysis is coordinated by the ego. But if we continuously *observe* the ego we will take up a truer discriminative position.

People generally live their lives by a standard, which they think is correct based on the views of others, which are imposed upon them from birth. These standards alter from community to community. We can therefore see immediately that there is little common ground in all societies on this planet when it comes to morals.

Moreover, being too moralistic can be the cause of reaching the end of our life thinking, "I should have done, said or thought this and I should not have done, said or thought that." This leaves a residue of dissatisfaction – often guilt – in the mind, which becomes karmic patterning in future lives.

We can raise our thinking above the level of this petty-analysis by unconditioning. We do this by stretching the ego rather than annihilating it. But stretching the ego does not mean growing it, any more than it means annihilating it. It means vaporising the ego so it can be seen through. When the ego is critically observed, rather than pandered to, we raise our consciousness to a higher, truer level and start to use our inbuilt natural quality – true discrimination.

We can be very one-sided with our opinions at times. In

deliberating this – which is a very useful exercise – it is possible to start clarifying where we are sometimes surprisingly, unnaturally, biased. Like regularly facing yourself, examining biased opinions on a frequent basis can help a great deal in unravelling the conditioning that causes our suffering.

The following areas of consideration may be useful but they are very limited and only quoted here to get you started in the process of using true discrimination. Add your own examples after you have thought more deeply about nature versus mankind's impositions and interference:

Personal greatness:

No person is greater than another, just as no tree or animal is greater than another. There is no need to look down or up to anyone. The lowly sloth might be just what you were like in a recent lifetime. In truth we are all one. You are actually in every other person, as well as every other object, to some extent or another.

Each of us has lifetimes of notable achievement and lifetimes of distress and many, many lifetimes in between these extremes. You cannot judge another's spiritual progress, nor can others judge yours. A dirty tramp coming along the road could be an enlightened master. A much praised leader could have a mind that is a curse to society. Both these extremes are exampled in our history books.

Interfering with nature:

Our planet will definitely reach extinction regardless of what any human being achieves. So, we could all concern ourselves more with our own evolution as a priority over what we think will happen to the planet.

Our planet itself makes no mistakes. If it becomes over populated then lessons are being learned. That is not to say you should give up trying, in whatever quest you chose to take on, whether it be for yourself or the planet. But use discrimination.

99.9% of the species that have ever inhabited this planet are already extinct. Nature ensures that none of them will survive, including mankind. Therefore you can't fight to keep the status quo or go back to 'old times'. Everything is moving on.

We all have to fight nature to survive. For example, we have to destroy nature to build homes. Can we say that developed countries should only have ever had a fraction of today's population volume? No, it's just the way the pace of life has taken us.

Restricting liberty:

Virtually all governmental dictate, including (e.g.) political correctness, helps nobody except the would-be controllers in their ability to squash personal freedom into an unrecognisable sludge. Governments invent all sorts of seemingly logical reasons why we need them to direct our affairs, and we believe them because we can't be bothered to *rationalise* – an important component of discrimination. For example, words like 'regulation' are used to disguise 'restriction'. We know this deep down but we don't react. We are too caught up in our problems in our little lives to view things from a bigger perspective.

Lack of self direction builds alarmingly quickly because we are not self-responsible. We allow ourselves to drift along presuming fairness is being dished out by others, as we think we would do if we were in the highest position of authority.

Likewise, who is to say that one person's idea of how things should be run is the correct one? It is spiritually offensive to force your opinions on to others. This offence deepens if this involves a restriction of another person's liberties. Of course, government workers have to earn an honest living, but there is no need to give up respect for each other.

We should treat each other as if we are each other. Many people (but not all) who seek or gain authoritative power should look very carefully – and urgently in my view – at their motives because, with their biased attitude, they could be digging themselves a very deep pit of burdensome karma for the future.

I apologise for touching on political strategy in a book of a spiritual genre. The reason is that the general populace seems very much asleep, accepting what they are told because they are busy sorting out the demands of the material life. With this materialistic preoccupation, it is understandable that people have become so lax at using their discriminative quality.

The above examples may seem a little strange if not controversial. If they do, I suggest you wake up and start thinking for yourself. There are countless other examples of how we have strayed from using our discriminative ability.

If you contemplate this matter for a while, discriminating what is real against what is made up by mankind, you will quickly notice how our world has become outlandishly subjective. And this is all done by us because of our gradual interment of our true nature to such a depth that we no longer want to face the truth.

The cardinal point here is that a refusal to discriminate properly will reinforce, even intensify, conditioning, and conditioning is the cause of our karmic build-up.

So, do you want to go backwards in an evolutionary sense, or forwards? The decision is yours. Going backwards is caused by (unfeasibly) resisting nature, which can only result in more suffering. Going forwards means flowing with nature, resulting in less suffering and more joy. Do make up your mind about this. Do it now!

What our senses perceive is unreal. If you don't rise above the petty rights and wrongs, and who says what about what and whom, you will miss the point of life altogether and be non-fulfilled at the end of it.

We are all capable of trying to go more with the flow of evolution rather than put our personal right or wrong view on to others. That is not to say lie back and be overrun by extremists. You should certainly get up and fight. But don't forget to fight first for your own development. Fight for your own unfoldment. Fight for your own opening up, your understanding of life. Fight to acknowledge your own faults and frailties.

Becoming self-reliant and self-accountable doesn't just advantage your individual life. It also helps the lives of our fellow humans far more than ideas of right and wrong. Self responsibility, *coupled with true discrimination*, builds immeasurable positive energy which radiates all around. This would help the planet and its communities benefit from the flow of nature, far more than trying to convince others about pet hates or ideas.

Relating To Non-Time

Come to terms with time! This has been the plea of both teachers and scientists who appeal to mankind to accept the truth of a multi-dimensional existence. I agree that accepting time for what it really is can enable the aspirant of self power, or the seeker of truth, to make rapid progress in their quest.

Time is the foremost component in the mind's imagination. Time is an abettor of the ego, allowing it to create images within the limits of our senses. Time makes us think that there is a yesterday and a tomorrow, a past moment and a future. It also gives us a false sense of separation, which is caused by solely focusing on three dimensions.

These truths about our existence have been highlighted scientifically since the 19th century, with growing intensity in the 20th century. Referring back to chapter 1, the three-dimensional sphere is not the foundation of existence.

What actually exists is oneness – multi-dimension-ness. All dimensions exist now. Everything is one, in one moment. Like a diamond, each face is a facet of the jewel and each appears to have different qualities, such as colours and sparkles caused by reflections, dependent upon the angle it is viewed from. Held afar it is recognisable as a diamond. But each face is not a diamond in itself. Nor are the faces of the diamond anything tangible, despite their seemingly observable colours.

Likewise, we have proven, by both mystical and scientific experience, that the three-dimensional realm is only an extremely limited aspect of all that is.

All dimensions exist here and now. Correspondingly, only one moment exists. If all dimensions are brought into consciousness there is no time, space or separation.

We will continue this vein of examination under the heading Non-Separation.

In one glimpse of pure consciousness, all truth is known. Until that recollection occurs there is much confusion about time.

When the limited three-dimensional consciousness is focused upon exclusively, the concept of past and present seem real. We need to bring out the stillness inside us to realise the folly of this trickery.

Many of my students have found it difficult to take a leap from the image of time to the truer image of non-time. To assist them, many have initially found it helpful to imagine standing in space far away from the planets; imagining they are taking the stance of a distant observer.

This image can help you appreciate the space-time relationship to which scientists continuously refer. For a start, the viewpoint of a distant observer highlights that there is no night or day, which inhabitants of earth live by. There are just pieces of rock, spinning around each other. Time starts to take on a new perspective from this viewpoint because the perceived planets can be observed as nothing else but motion (or vibration). One can acquire a sort of sixth sense during this exercise too – a sense that all energy moves and that energy is nothing but motion.

Naturally, one revolution of a planet, or the lifetime of a universe, still seems to take up what we call *time*. So does walking from the spot you are standing on to another place. However, if a universe was observed fron the outside, a completely new reaction would arise from the question, "What time is it?"

Motion happens now. We are always experiencing now. Yesterday and tomorrow are ideas in our minds based on memory and projection. Both memory and projection are thought patterns, which are not real. They are strings of words made up in our heads based on the fundamentally wrong presumption that matter is the whole of existance.

When you sense non-time's greater reality you can further your appreciation about the three dimensional sphere not being a stands-on-its-own actuality, but more a sort of dense reflection – an identifier – of multi-dimensional existence.

So, time as a concept is limited to the framework of unreality observed by the senses, which are also limited and therefore not totally real.

Some readers may conjecture, at this point, that this theory is fascinating, but that a gigantic, seemingly impossible change of thought patterning is needed to move from the concept of being a limited human being to acquiring knowledge of the oneness of their actuality.

To counter this, remember that the whole of the consciousness of actuality is operating in you right now, closer to you than your eyelid is to your eye. It is within and throughout every cell of your being and within and throughout every thought.

It is not a big step to open the curtains just a tiny bit to let in a little light. Nobody will draw back the curtains for themselves in one sweep. Would you willingly awaken yourself from a long, long sleep with a spotlight and a siren?

More thought given to the non-reality of time and space is a good place to commence letting in a tiny bit of light, as I have phrased it. The more you study concepts of truth, the more you will awaken.

So, in reality, time is an imagination. Only one moment exists. After affirming this fact, and accepting that solid matter is an unreal fragmentation of a higher dimensional reality, the recognition starts to dawn, in an extremely still mind, that nothing whatsoever is happening in this three dimensional sphere. There is no journey here at all, either with a beginning or an end. Wholeness is infinite. Limitation is unreal.

Getting What You Want Using Subtle Energy

"You can get everything you like if you develop yourself to a stage to be able to demand it. Deserve first, then demand and everything you like will come running to you... You'll have control of nature and the whole of nature supports you."

– Gururaj

Becoming aware of the whole self – whatever picture you might have of it in the beginning – is three quarters of the proficiency needed in accomplishing a position of self-power, happiness and fulfilment. This position can include abilities to develop new qualities and / or acquire material stuff if that is your choice.

Such a possibility emerges because you release yourself from the bondage of the human mind and opening up higher channels of connection to all other things, people, qualities and opportunities – to all 'higher' energies.

I have encountered many people who, at their first reaction, are resistant to material gain (by manipulation). Most of these people were affected by misappropriated guilt or thoughts of being judged or needing to be seen to be good – and the like.

Others could not see wealth and material gain as a positive energy – which it is when *used positively*. But they all at least, after opening themselves up to subtle energy attunement, had a bit of fun with the arrival of increased resourcefulness which occurred 'accidentally' to almost all of them from day one of committing themselves to personal unfoldment.

I couldn't possibly count the number of instances of procurement I have witnessed or heard about, often to the amazement of the participants who were often not intending to procure anything in the first place! They range from speedily finding a parking space in unlikely circumstances to being bestowed with items of substantial value within hours of thinking about them.

Almost every procurement involves visualisation. Visualisation can be learned in minutes, despite various schools charging a small fortune for the instruction. The person who is more integrated with their higher self can achieve much more than one who isn't. Expensive courses on visualisation can be a waste of money if the student is locked tightly within the framework of the three-dimensional thinking process.

The parking space tactic never ceases to amaze me, after 40 years of my continuous use of it. I could quote examples of all sorts of procurements that happen to people, on a daily basis sometimes. To get numbers into perspective, I am probably talking millions of occurrences by now rather than thousands, just from the few thousand people that have been taught meditation and allied practices via instruction in which I have been involved.

The list is endless. On a wider scale, users often change their bad habits of a lifetime, cure themselves of disease, and even acquire houses or luxury items they never dreamed at one time would come into their possession.

I don't want to give the impression that I am trying to teach mankind to find happiness via the attainment of material stuff using mind control. Having stated this, I am aware that, at first glance, the majority of readers wouldn't object to having powers for accumulating more personal comfort. The short end of this is to unequivocally state that everybody has these powers all through their life, but few bother to use them.

Anyhow, procurement is not just about acquiring material stuff but is more often about changing ourselves for the better. Handled in the right way, procurement is a positive activity because it usually involves effort, it involves self-direction and it includes self responsibility, self accountability and self-reliance.

First, you must appreciate that material stuff comes and goes. This is a law of nature. Secondly, you must accept that gaining material stuff will not necessarily produce a pleasant outcome. A fairly transparent example here is to think of hankering after a Rolls Royce, and acquiring one by whatever means. Then the car has an accident, possibly fatal, that a smaller car could have avoided.

So, material gain is not the be all and end all of life. The ultra-rich are the first to confirm this fact. The acme of comfort brings with it a level of convenience rather than happiness.

Nevertheless, why live on sandwiches if feasts are available?

I acknowledge the fact that some folks get stuck for a while in the desire to access material gain for the sake of material gain. The mind can convince you for a while that material stuff or money will bring happiness by providing a cushion against life's more painful demands.

I don't consider this an altogether bad thing because material gain leads to an acknowledgement of the *extreme limitation of material stuff.* Ask any billionaire. The rich soon discover that they want answers to life rather than more and more wealth. Many of them, of course, only realise this when they are approaching their demise. What a waste of life, I often think, for a person to have acquired masses of earthly stuff and not have the faintest idea how to progress with their evolution after leaving the body.

So, goal-orientated material gain can be a positive step on the path to unfoldment, provided the goal is aimed at self development. Get as much from using the law of attraction as you wish but don't treat material stuff as the priority. Don't get attached to it or you'll be frightened to be parted from it. If you become glued to the notion of wanting more and more, you will simply lead yourself into a pit of confusion.

If you prioritise opening yourself up to vibrational feeling – beyond solid matter – then you'll enjoy everything to the maximum and come to know that you don't die at all. What could be more joyful in life?

For those in genuine need, procurement of basic essentials is obviously a great help. There is absolutely no problem in focusing on your idea of higher energy to demand what you really need. I have found, for myself and others, genuine needs are met quite quickly when calling on subtle energy to intervene.

It helps to visualise what will result from you being helped. This is because a flow of energy will always enable the universe to help you, as opposed to a one-off happening commensurate with your desires that has no extended purpose.

For instance, if you needed food you could visualise food

coming to you, then eating it, then your body remaining healthy, which would result in you becoming more positive in your outlook and actions – and possibly that others will benefit by your better state of health too. Any positive on-flowing outlook is good, related to the consequences of gaining material stuff, and it helps you acquire what is needed.

Apart from intense visualisation, I have known a number of people, some of whom practiced balance and alignment techniques and some who didn't, to simply ask the 'universal force' (and other such expressions) to provide a whole host of things for their needs – and it works! Sometimes it works instantly. Try it, if you haven't already. It doesn't work every time, and not in specific time frame, even for the well-practised, but it is not harmful if you go about it in an unselfish manner. This procedure is more aligned to the Shakti method mentioned in Chapter 3.

Commitment to unfolding yourself to your higher vibrations will help enormously in respect of drawing things to you that you want. When you genuinely open yourself up to the idea that you are part of everything and not a separate, controlled individual, you start helping yourself from a higher, more subtle level.

We will touch on prosperity consciousness a little later, so as to refine further the subject of material gain.

If you are being positive about your life and respecting your duty to yourself by unfolding beyond the confines of the human mind, you are not likely to overdo material acquisition to the point of being destructive to yourself or others.

My four basic tenets, in this respect, are:
- never knowingly do harm to another person or their property;
- be aware of, and respectful of, the whole Self – 24 hours a day if possible;
- when calling on subtle energy use it positively (not least, negative use will rebound on the user multi-fold);
- be exceedingly vigilant with thoughts relating to the three principles above.

Let's now refer to more subtle (and more powerful) changes that an individual might desire, rather than dallying any longer in thoughts of procuring objects of one's choice.

For instance, the reader may prefer to contemplate becoming a more radiant, confident, bold, fearless or capable person. Whatever your particular desire in this respect, it is a more arduous to change old patternings of fear, low-esteem, guilt, feeling lonely and the like than learning to command a parking space or piece of furniture.

Unfoldment is the process of reaching some stage of self-integration by means of freeing yourself from the bondage the mind exerts. By unfolding yourself you release yourself. By unfolding yourself your higher consciousness comes more into play systematically.

The more a person unfolds, the more they will find that their values change. The far reaching consequence, as balance emerges naturally, is that the integrated individual finds that they don't actually need more material stuff to make themselves happy. Nor do they need major changes in personality to be able to reach realisation of the Self. These stages fall into the category of *degrees of realisation*.

The greatest benefit you can attain from visualisation is to visualise yourself becoming more open, positive, non-judgemental etc. with the knowledge of your Real Self infiltrating into you. This will bring a million-fold more benefits in your evolution than any type of material acquisition.

Finally I should caution that most people visualise to some extent without knowing it. We all lead ourselves to goals by projecting a picture in our minds of how we see ourselves in the future. This is what I term *mild* visualisation. But some people visualise intensely without accounting for what they intend to do as a result of achieving a goal.

Take the example of a celebrity or a jackpot winner who attained fortune quickly, even if by sheer drive and determination, and subsequently wrecked their life because of all the trappings they acquired. This chain of events would occur because the person's mind projection of their fame or fortune *did not contain sufficient detail of what positive response could take place as a result of achieving their goal.*

So, visualisation is a prime example of the need for thought control. Always be wary of the possible aftermath of acquiring something you desire and take that into account in what you are commanding from the universe. Then you can balance your approach to the subject of procurement and to your use of whatever you draw to yourself.

The mechanics of visualisation are expanded upon in the Appendices.

7

Practical Ways and Means

Additional Attunement
Self-Strengthening Principles

Unconditioning releases you from the cunning and masterful mind, which has us all enslaved.

Because unconditioning is a cleansing action, as opposed to reconditioning, it is *not* brain washing (or auto-suggestion). As you *unlearn* you don't change to a different set of beliefs. What happens is *you become less burdened with mind-stuff*. In this process the natural flow of inner subtle energy emerges more and more.

I strongly advise that you continually carry out the exercise of uncovering yourself (by facing yourself), and that you bring true discrimination more and more into daily life. By doing this, you will discover endless little lies you have been telling yourself in order to get yourself by in this world. These self deceptions are hidden in your conditioning. The more you face the truth about yourself, the more you'll unfold.

Presently, you probably project pictures of what you are and how the universe fits together using mental images of solid matter, because the mind has built within itself its own relative standards of perception.

The analysis that goes on in that invisible, calculating network is awesome. Every tiny little thing that is seen, heard, touched, tasted or smelled is fitted into a snapshot library containing about three billion exposures in each lifetime.

But you need to rid yourself of these fairy-tale limitations and open up new knowledge – actual knowledge. Uncovering yourself is like opening a series of previously indiscernible doors in a corridor whose distant end is the permanent state of happiness you've always wanted.

Thoughts occur by the thousands every day, related to images in the snapshot library. Thereby imagination is formed based on what we sense is time and space. This is how we build our projections, judgements, likes and dislikes etc., all stuck into a lidded pot where the past is the structure of the pot and the future is an escape route via the lid.

In short, the mind is an individual viewpoint based on reactions to memory. It is a package of energy vibrations, conjured up like a mirage within its limited confines, which presumes a sense of its own space, of separation, of importance.

Meditate and Let Go

You may readily allude, so far, to a feeling that the solution to all our problems is in overcoming our false sense of separate-ness. Yet this often combines with a fear that letting go of the *safety in separation* is almost impossible to contemplate. Face this fear and you will find that it is unfounded, and you will soon catapult yourself to new joy.

First you need to find peace of mind. You can do this by using the letting go process. It's a matter of loosening your grip from that which you are unnecessarily attached.

Don't worry. I am not suggesting you to dump your individuality while you want to hang on to it. You are not going to throw yourself off a cliff. Letting go is largely a purging of your worries. It is not a process of giving up anything at all.

Practicing balance and alignment techniques, of which meditation is singularly important, will unendingly assist the letting go process. The main change that occurs in a person who meditates regularly is that the analytical whirling in the mind slows down.

From a practical viewpoint, your inner self is totally at peace. Each session of 'blanking' the mind allows a tiny amount of this ultimate stillness to permeate into the busy surface thinking.

This results in a less entangled mind, which is a more natural mind. A mind full of junk is not a natural mind. It's a self-developed imposition that causes suffering.

By letting go, a balancing effect quickly impregnates the thinking process, such that anxiety lessens. The nuts and bolts description is that the frontal lobe of the brain, which produces self consciousness and emotions, and the parietal lobe – responsible for relating sensory input to our imagined location of individuality – both attenuate their activity.

Every sane person can meditate. Some folk don't attempt it because they inappropriately pre-conceive that a calm approach, which they possibly don't have, is a prerequisite. This is not so.

During meditation the mind does not actually blank off except for the occasional millisecond. Practical meditation, other than that practised by devotees, monks etc., is a process of dealing with thoughts, mostly thoughts that don't really matter.

Regular meditation helps to infuse the natural, pure energy flow into the mind and subdues the wasted energy activity which causes self-limitations. Since the mechanics of meditation is to allow thoughts to dispel without anxiety, the participant also brings this conceptualisation more and more into play in daily life.

The over simplified descriptions of meditation, found in many publications, are not helpful in my view. I see countless examples in the media. For example (possibly following a relaxation technique), "Sit quietly and concentrate only on your breathing." This is not an instruction on how to meditate efficiently.

In correct meditation you should *not* concentrate, despite the technique bolstering your ability to concentrate better in the normal waking state. Possibly, the authors of such bitty information have their readers' interests at heart. But I often think they are trying to fill up space in their articles without proper research.

Proper effective meditation is so very simple to do. Proper meditation deals with thoughts by *quietly* dispelling them while allowing them their existence rather than attempting to obliterate thoughts or bar them.

If you attempt meditation by one of the hundreds of ill-informed instruction methods you will fail to achieve the potential benefits. You could thereby be put off, consequently losing out on the tremendous potential advantages.

I have very little time for recordings of rain, musical sounds, etc. I have questioned many suppliers of such cosy little mind-numbings and not one of them seemed to know anything about true yogic objectives. They mostly appear to be selling, often at considerable cost, little experiences and escape routes that remind me of driving into a cul-de-sac for a rest; then having to drive back out to continue the same arduous journey.

Correct techniques are structured to deal with your thoughts in such a way that you solve your life by natural growth. You move on.

You cease to analyse as much as you did previously. You become the observer of thoughts. Then impressions start to dissipate. You don't eradicate them. You move on from them. And that's why a truly quietened mind is said to be the ultimate tool that melts away karma.

It's a matter of personal choice of course. Not everyone desires to move on. But if you want to change life for the better there is no choice but to move on. We'll discuss this further shortly.

Proper meditation helps you to replace the strangulated, solid-matter thinking process with a more natural one. This can have the following benefits, as well as those already mentioned:

- reduction in high blood pressure,
- better health all round,
- ability to deal with everyday challenges,
- better intuition and creativity,
- improved relationships,
- a more contented and confident personality,
- improve longevity potential
- improved ability to focus on the task in hand.

What happens in a practical sense, as a result of correct meditation, is that the conscious mind starts to respond differently to input. The synaptic control between the left and right hemispheres of the brain modifies itself into a better state of balance.

In essence, your mind 'lets go' of the millions of impressions that have built up. It doesn't need to hang on to them any longer when the ego becomes less dominant.

Millions of people literally think themselves to death by blocking the flow of the inner self. Such blocking is an unconscious activity, but it is an activity that consumes vital life-supporting forces. Frequently, a derivative of blocking is the onset of disease.

Life-extension programmes incorporating letting go techniques are becoming increasingly successful as a medical treatment because they focus on the centre of a person's make up. Balancing the inner core of you is more effective for your health than fire-fighting physical ailments.

By letting go you, metaphorically speaking, stand on the cliff face and push away from you that very (negative) force that is trying to drag you over it. You are also inviting into your life your whole universal make up, which is life-giving and not life-consuming.

You also become better at letting go of your projections and expectations when you improve your natural discrimination between useless and useful thoughts. Concurrently, this calms your emotions. You become less attached to what you think might happen in the future.

We have looked at several examples of 'hanging on' – the opposite of letting go – under the subject of discrimination. Unwillingness to let go of past impressions is based on the assumption in your mind that, by moving on from old thinking patterns, nothing better than your past or present experiences will emerge.

In summary, letting go relieves unnecessary mental pressure by unblocking and modifying the thinking process. Most people spend their whole lives enslaved to a limited system (of authority and limited achievement) not knowing that, by stepping aside from what they previously considered to be right thinking, they could draw to themselves a whole host of treasures that would lead to a satisfying and happy life.

Letting go is not a process of losing your grip on anything tangible. It simply helps to change your perspective, which in turn alters your samskaric patterning that is built on past thoughts and experiences. You're breaking into the self-feeding spiral that has had you held down for lifetime after lifetime. You liberate yourself from the imprisoning element of the mind.

Non-Expectation

"Expectation is the father of disappointment, and disappointment is the mother of suffering."

– Gururaj

The preceding quotation speaks entirely for itself. So much of our suffering comes from our disappointments. The direct inference here is that if you don't have expectations you cannot be disappointed.

"Why should I not expect things to happen?" – you might exclaim.

It is totally pointless to wallow in expectation because nothing in life whatsoever is certain – not even your next breath.

You could argue this point by saying that the sun will definitely be coming up tomorrow to bring the daylight once more. But even that presumption is not certain. One day this planet could explode or implode. It definitely will not be here at some point. That day could be today. It is not difficult to imagine human life being wiped away in a day, given the capability of present day weapons or the knowledge we already have of asteroids and super volcanoes.

Nothing is certain. So why don't you live with this idea, get used to it and consequently start to live in the flow of life – which changes all the time – rather than *expect* things to be the same, or of some particular result your mind expects, tomorrow?

Your burdens and your negative thoughts hold you in self-limitation. However, the limitation can be reduced dramatically as soon as you start to flow with life – living the present moment without expectation.

Expectation has other relatives too. Risk-avoidance is one of its cousins. When you encompass risk, rather than try to avoid it, all sorts of possibilities open up.

When you hanker after a fixed result your potential is thwarted. Whatever we project to be a *certain* outcome of a plan is a picture on a screen in our mind – a sort of fantasy. But the future is not only uncertain, it is unreal. If you contemplate the matter of non-time or less limited consciousness, it is simple to accept that nothing is real. Therefore nothing should be expected.

What we need to do is stop struggling to formulate a set of circumstances that we *think* will answer our quest for happiness. This struggle produces an endless string of disappointments.

Everything you need for happiness is in this moment. If your circumstances are such that you are feeling distress, then change something. But don't project the final outcome. Plan and forget. If a plan goes astray then re-plan and forget. Get in the flow by utilising non-expectation as an adjunct to your active life of conscious effort and positive thinking. With that, you have a formula for success in any area of life.

Using non-expectation as a tool does *not* mean you should shrug your shoulders at life and give up the attempt to accomplish things. Quite the reverse is true. Non-expectation stops you wasting mental energy by being too attached to a *specific* outcome from your efforts. When you stop being too attached, the end result is frequently better than originally visualised.

Awareness

"There's no difference between instinct, intuition and awareness.
It is just a matter of degrees in our development in life."

– Gururaj

Greater awareness is another essential quality in our quest to improve our intuitiveness-to-logic ratio.

True awareness is being able to focus on one object or subject while, at the same time, being aware of everything around you in the environmental surroundings (without giving any of it particular attention). This is *not* as difficult to achieve as it may sound.

We are usually blinkered to most of what is happening around us, even close to us. We are taken up with our immediate necessities and desires which keep our mind pattern stolid.

This preoccupation represents the same sort of patterning as our consciousness. We have whole consciousness built in to us but we don't exploit its potential. Likewise, we have the potential of total awareness but we are missing it.

When we become fully aware we become fully conscious. Therefore, improving awareness helps to unfold degrees of consciousness.

What happens when we expand awareness is that we become much better at seeing everything at once, including ourself and our life within its greater, truer context. Right brain activity flourishes. Acceptance becomes more prevalent. The out-of-control spiral of judging right and wrong eases. We become more truly discriminative, comparing the real to the unreal.

The practicality of improving awareness is that it acts like a pressure relief valve. It also develops our ability to see the big picture – whether we are encountering a problem or our personal position relating to something else – thereby assisting us in solving difficult, often longstanding, dilemmas.

Awareness also helps release the mind from its imprisoned status, thereby engendering more possibilities and greater potential.

An essential ingredient of awareness is observation. By becoming the observer you abundantly assist yourself with reducing stress and fear. You live more *in* the world, but not *of* the world. Moreover, you increasingly see the world through other people's eyes as well as your own, the result of which is a complaisant understanding of others' opinions.

Being open to the views of others helps self examination, and so on. All these attunement practices underscore each other. They knit together in a web of self-support via perspective reorientation.

You can test your current awareness level in almost any location. For example, are you aware of your feet touching the ground or your backside being in touch with the seat you are sitting on?

You may think these questions strange or simplistic at first. They refer to such simple, everyday things. However, when you expand on such illustrations you will see how little your awareness of your own body is generally taking place. This demonstrates that most awareness of more distant things is on the basis of analysis or spatial assessment rather than intuitiveness or creativity.

Here is another helpful activity. To start to rejuvenate true awareness, take a short walk down any street. Observe the buildings in fine detail. Keep walking and try to take in every detail of everything you see – people, vehicles, the roadway itself, the sky, flowers and plant life (including the grass and trees), gateways, fences, colours and forms, *everything*. It takes very little time to become adept at this.

The brain has an endless capacity to take in observed data. You are not going to clog up the thinking mechanism so long as you are not analysing. In fact you unclog your brain because you'll not be involved with the constant rough-house of the ego. Just observe, but try not to miss anything out.

The same exercise can apply when in a shop, office or any other room. Observe all the shapes, colours and fabrics, what everyone is doing related to each other, even the shape and number of the light fittings, floor coverings, desks or moveable objects, every detail possible. Get used to doing this type of exercise as much as possible, without analysis, until it becomes more or less continuous. When it becomes second nature, it will be effortless.

Being thoroughly aware, in an observing, *non-analytical* manner, is a superb unconditioning tool. Pure awareness is the state where you are aware of everything simultaneously. Total knowingness is knowledge of the universal mind – which cannot be analysed by logical thinking.

Another way to describe this is that superconsciousness infiltrates the individual consciousness. When you are totally aware, you develop a total affinity to everything. You move away from the perpetual 'I and You' perspective. You come to regard everyone and everything as a unity. Non-separation becomes more a reality rather than just an idea.

Contemplation
"Meditation leads to a concentrated, unfragmented mind and a concentrated mind leads to success in contemplation. Contemplation is the crowning glory in mysticism."
— Gururaj

Contemplation is a masterful spiritual practice. It is the art of letting thoughts flow. You touch on this practice during correctly performed meditation.

Contemplation is an advanced form of meditation. Meditation seeks thought moderation by allowing thought to disperse itself. Contemplation *encourages* thought without concentration or attachment. It is undirected thought, where thoughts are observed as a continuous flow, as smooth as oil running out of a container.

The secret of achieving this wonderful free flow of thoughts, which doesn't affect your mind at all, is to pick out the beginning and the end of each thought and to ignore the middle.

This may sound a bit ridiculous if not incredulous. But it is an art. Like any form of art, the more you do it the better you become at it. One thought flows from another to another, in a stream, without your emotions getting caught up in any reaction to the thoughts. You might not be too successful at this until you have become reasonably adept at meditating. Even then, it will take persistence to become skilled.

Correct contemplation not only helps to clear up your anxieties, it also helps dissolve your karma because you allow yourself a pure flow with nature.

Furthermore, there is no barrier to thought in contemplation. Therefore, in this process, thoughts that occur can be inspiring or revealing or, again, problem solving. The main confusion associated with problems is that the mind gets caught up in a cul-de-sac, whirring around and around. In contemplation so many thoughts can flow through you that there is a good chance they can lead to solutions that would otherwise elude you.

In contemplation you are totally absorbed. Although the thought is undirected it is powerfully focusing, without reaction. By using this practice regularly you can therefore vastly improve your efficiency in almost anything during your daily activities.

Not least, contemplation improves the profundity of your meditation. You get to go deeper without interruption. By this means you access more and more of your universal self because you resist it less. You come to allow the flow of nature to take over without you being fearful of losing anything.

Spiritual Masters, who are able to enter the state of unity consciousness at will, use contemplation to traverse the whole range of the universal mind, within minutes. They move from the embodied ego, which contains billions of thoughts, to nothingness (in terms of consciousness) in one straight move.

Nothing keeps a fully self-realised human being contained within any thought while he/she crosses the whole sphere of thought that has ever been, in every dimension. Thought just flows through and flows away, to reveal the nothingness that is actual existence. Contemplation is the perfect meditation and vice versa.

So, we have come full circle. The human mind has access to pure consciousness in every thought it ever thinks but the activity of the mind – the involvement in thought – produces cloudiness which acts like thick veil; an opaque screen. Meditation and attunement de-fragment the mind and allow the restoration of its concentrative powers. The ultra-strong mind is the key that allows access to our inner self, our (lost) inner power. Perfect balance in the mind is the key. The ego is still there but it is mastered. The mind becomes a servile tool.

Boldness and Fearlessness

The letting go process is fortified when we overcome fear. Many people are constantly fearful. Fears constitute projections of, for example, being hurt, being judged by others, being disliked, being unloved, fear of losing things or close ones, fear of potential failure, being broke, becoming ill and, most of all, fear of death. The list of fears is a long one.

But what is fear? Fear is the opposite of love. Fear stops the natural flow of life-supporting energy, both subtle and physical. Fear is one of the most negative energies that it is possible to invoke.

Almost every fear stems from the fear of death. The ego dominates with the idea that the little self is the centre of all and should be preserved ad infinitum. The ego has to do this because it is not real and it is aware of its own upcoming extinction at the point of bodily demise, and so tries to convince the intellect that the same applies to the wholeness of the personality.

Fear can be resolved to a large extent if the correct mental attitude towards death and life can be attained.

With a strong, concentrated mind it is possible to release oneself from the stranglehold of the idea of 'me and mine' and replace it with 'thee and thine.'

Admittedly, this phrase could conjure up the idea of a personal god somewhere. But it's not meant to. It's more about thinking of life as a necessary experience and an offering to the one-ness of all – which is the *actual* you. In this way we can use our mind to counterbalance fear, which holds us on the sparse side of a massive blockage affecting our progression and achievements.

The short solution to becoming fearless is to *use* fear.

How does one use fear to overcome fear? The answer to this question is ludicrously uncomplicated. I agree with those who advise teaching children this technique, so as to help them minimise fear in adult life.

To use fear we have to *feel* fear, not be frightened of fear or try to avoid fear. We are not actually frightened of fear, but that cunning mind tells us we are, so we keep away from the emotions that cause fear if we possibly can.

Paradoxically, this is exactly the approach that causes us to be fearful. To reiterate, we are not frightened of fear, we project that fear is going to destabilise us, whereas *facing* fear is actually going to strengthen us.

It's like evoking the well-known adage, "feel the fear and do it anyway," in every fearful situation. There's an excellent best selling book with this title, by Susan Jeffers.

When a little trepidation is faced and felt, fear can be dispelled by going ahead with whatever we are fearful of. We sometimes have to summon up bravery to solve the uncomfortable emotion of a situation, but meditation and attunement practices can help you solve that problem.

The more the 'feeling fear' approach is practised, the more the projection of fear dilutes. Boldness builds and fear is put into its rightful perspective.

"Fear nothing – and be brave," was Gururaj's constant, imploring command to his chelas, in order that they could realise their Real Self.

There are all kinds of situations where boldness is either need-ed or desired. Examples are taking on responsibilities, a major turn-ing-point in life, approaching somebody new, confronting awk-ward situations, taking risks, losing someone, even helping someone. There are numerous other examples too.

If you ever want to summon up boldness, Say to yourself, "'Give me one good reason why I should not be bold, *if* I am not attached to the end result." Being attached to the end result not only causes fear and restricts boldness; it also severely limits your potential.

After I first heard this little tip, I put this instruction to the test on countless occasions and found it to be remarkably helpful.

Becoming bolder, which you can do by practice, will solve lots of situations which make you uncomfortable or restless and will also pave the way to acquiring what you want. It also helps you become less self-conscious.

I will not go into assertiveness here. There are countless relevant courses of instruction widely available. Obviously assertiveness in the right place at the right time is a very practical adjunct to being bold and fearless.

There is plenty of detailed literature on becoming fearless generally available too. Few would disagree with the advisability of studying therapeutic methods to reduce fear.

Confrontation

Intertwined with the ability to overcome fearfulness is the indispensable virtuosity of dealing with confrontation.

If we steer away from confrontation, which many of us do, we deny ourselves the opportunity to dismantle mind-induced barriers. We also miss the opportunity to expand our personal potential.

We often allow others to say what is disagreeable to us without confronting the disagreement. This also applies to others doing disagreeable things or trying to get away with outcomes we are not happy with, etc. The result is that we moan about disagreeable people or outcomes. Situations are left unsatisfactory because of our failure to confront.

Dealing with confrontation is simple. You just have to put in some conscious effort. You need to decide that you are going to confront every issue that crops up in day to day life. This could simply involve dealing with a shopkeeper or perhaps someone on the telephone who will not agree to your request or your required terms. It could relate to challenging somebody who is continuously allowed to steal social conversation. It could be a person who has been rude in an encounter, however small or large. It could be a pestering annoyance from someone quite close to you. I'm sure you can think of examples in your day to day life.

To counteract a resistance to confrontation, each person can develop their own phrases with which they are comfortable. I'm not implying there won't be a sense of discomfort to some extent or another. That is part of confrontation. But I have found the following method to be helpful to virtually everyone I know who uses it.

The open secret of succeeding at confrontation is *further examination*. When something occurs which you do not agree with, but you would rather circumvent the matter so as not to cause offence, make an instant decision to go for further examination.

Of equal import, this can nearly always be done by turning the subject towards yourself instead of the perpetrator of your annoyance. Doing this largely dispels the awkwardness you are feeling.

In practical terms this means steering away from starting a confrontation with the attitude, "this (or you) is totally absurd". That can come later if necessary!

The easy approach is to first direct comments towards yourself, about you. For example the "I have a problem with that" avoids an immediate knee-jerk reaction in the person you are confronting because it is not directed at them, it is directed at you. This also takes the sting out of the direct-fight emotional feeling welling up in (you) the confronter. And it keeps the resistance of the person you are confronting at a low level.

Then you can continue with a reason, viz, "I still have a problem with that *because* ..." Then keep going and going until your viewpoint is respected, when an even basis for further discussion will have been reached.

Lastly, do not seek the end of the confrontation too quickly. Think to yourself, "I want this to go on as long as necessary to get my point validated." This attitude not only avoids the other person getting their way unfairly, but also increases the chance that the other person will come to respect your view because they are either uncomfortable with the confrontation or are becoming convinced that you have a valid point.

It is much a matter of boldness. Equally it can be a game of dare in which you can have fun pressing your point home. One point worth bearing in mind is that you should back down if you discover you are wrong during the confrontation. In such circumstances, if you emphasise your apology, you will not lose face, you will gain respect. And, the person you have confronted is going to admire your forthrightness.

Practicing confrontation is a worthwhile step towards eradicating fear. So, why not brave it? It is a physical process that will come to satisfy you tremendously when you make a habit of it.

Taking Risks

"One has to abandon forever the search for security and reach out to the risk of living with both arms. One has to embrace life like a lover."

– Morris West

Taking risks is something often thought of as a no-go area. But, again, we can overcome our inbuilt fears of risk if we readjust our feeling of 'little-self' importance. By doing so we have further opportunity to dissolve some barriers and increase self-potential.

In the Serenity Prayer, quoted earlier in this book (under Change), the aspirant seeks courage. But so often we find ourselves lacking courage because we also seek security.

Seeking security can seriously limit our achievements. This may sound like a perplexity but is there really such a thing as security? Ask this question to any person on their deathbed and you will get a rational answer. Those who are close to death nearly always reflect that to have taken more risks would have opened up their life to more possibilities.

Risk is mostly avoided because of the predominance of fears

and insecurities. The spiritual path, the evolutionary path, is a gamble – although gamble is not really the appropriate word. The appropriate wording would be to describe that you 'have to take a chance into the unknown sphere of which you know nothing'. And to take that chance into the unknown sphere where you know nothing, *you will find everything*. It requires courage, because of your conditioning. Therefore it is said by all Masters that the spiritual path is the hero's path.

Don't be scared to make wrong decisions. Learning comes to us from mis-takes. Learning does not come to us from doing everything we have always done and not branching out. Nor does reward. There is no such thing as failure – there is only learning followed by success.

The consequence of most bad decisions can be rectified. The consequence of not going out on a limb is that fruit, which all grows out on limbs and branches – not on trunks – cannot be gathered. Rewards come after the risk, and not the other way around.

Is risk natural or does it have to be forced? Risk is natural. When you observe a young child, its nature is to take risks at almost every step. Even learning to walk in the first place involves much risk – and every child loves it!

Yes, our nature is to reach out, to explore, and to go beyond the present boundary. It is only the constant pressure on us from older people, especially when we are young, that instils in us the idea that taking risks is generally unsafe.

Author Andrew Matthews, in Being Happy!, wrote (edited):

"Those who become preoccupied with being safe and secure so often spend their evenings spellbound by doses of soaps and sitcoms while their own lives degenerate into a parade of one boring year after the next.

"In loving and caring we risk. Saying 'I love you' can be a risky business, but the rewards can be fantastic. Being different is risky too but it also means you can be yourself.

"The universe is continually encouraging us to stretch out, to climb to be extraordinary.

"Every winner takes on the risk of losing. Each of us loses at times but the more risk we partake in the more wins we will eventually have – even after strings of losses. A game of bowls involves the risk of losing, but it is the partaking and the fun it creates that adds richness to life."

If you observe the risks you take daily without realising it, such as crossing the road, getting married, starting a new job or business, eating out, travelling, even climbing the stairs, etc., etc., you are less likely to think you will advantage yourself by trying to 'play it safe'.

Moving On

Before you start unfolding yourself, your self-imposed patterning binds you to limitation. When you bring about changes which free off these restrictions, some of the changes will have been looked upon as welcome and some not so welcome. What seems unwelcome, by way of change, is due to (unnecessary) attachment.

As stated previously, everything in the physical universe changes. No matter what satisfaction with your Earth-bound status quo you may have established at any one time, the present circumstances are a transitory, fleeting moment. Even if your achievements with personal love, material assets, status and comforts appeases you, enthrals you or simply contents you right now you will soon see change coming about.

A self-resolve concept that can help build your self empowerment *instantly* is the notion of moving on. Yes, this does involve stepping through the portals of acceptance and change. It is a practical, day-to-day opportunity to highlight these important would-be barriers, which can be cleared in a practical way once your determination to accept and welcome change becomes established.

Moving on is inevitable. When you become positive about it, you instantly remove so many of the rust-bound shackles that bind you to limitation and suffering. So, why not get positive about it today?

Your *attitude* to prospective change is what counts. If you simply rationalise, "This will all change, I do not hold any importance as to the *timing* of that change," you will flourish like never before. You will feel uplifted. This is another way of operating attachment in a non-attached way.

Correspondingly, if you try to go back – to reconstruct a previous set of circumstances, which gave you temporary satisfaction – you are unlikely to succeed and you will deplete yourself of much vital energy. Everything moves on. It's best to get in the flow of this principle.

The nature inside you – the one pure consciousness – is always homing in on the origin. You cannot successfully fight against this tide. You cannot succeed in making the impermanent permanent. So many folk suffer because they don't accept this fact of nature.

If you imagine ever-changing nature to be an unstoppable rolling juggernaut, you may be able to depict yourself lying in the road trying to stop the juggernaut by raising your finger in the air. There you are, lying in the road, having built a little temporary nest of stuff around you because you are convinced that what you see at close quarters is all that keeps you safe and comfortable. You're aware of the juggernaut rolling towards you but continue to live your life as if you might be able to halt it.

Why don't you go juggernauting? You can sit in the driving seat if you want to. The juggernaut is definitely going to roll on, so you might as well get on board and have fun with what is going to happen next on the journey. If you take this positive stance willingly, you'll not only experience a carnival atmosphere but you'll also remove your fears and worries as you go along.

Can moving on be uncomfortable? Certainly it can, if you obey the ego at the same time you are trying to put it in its correct place. This sometimes happens in the early stages of self unfoldment, when the mind is not used to the idea that ego is a made-up phenomena. But this soon passes as the new (more real) angles of perception settle in.

Also, feelings of vulnerability or unassuredness can occur. All this is referred to as 'growth' because, when the subtle mind is becoming more established, it's like *growing* a new perspective. Nothing is growing at all really because everything in the universe is fully established in you already. It's the ego, trying to reinforce your samskaric patterning, which causes conflict. Once again, you have to insist that you are something more than your ego in order to get the ego to settle into a more translucent, controllable form.

If you go through a stage where you really don't like the unconditioning process you can always take a break from it. Your inner energy will guide you correctly as to how much unconditioning you want to do. During such periods in my own unfolding process I have continued with a focal gazing technique and subtle energy breathing at least once each day.

Reading from the works of a true master helps tremendously too, because your understanding grows when you continually point your mind to something uplifting rather than to sensory input.

I suggest you bookmark the previous four or five paragraphs so that you can refer back to them at any time of inner unrest.

What unfailingly accompanies a positive attitude towards moving on is the eventual discovery that new ground is more satisfying than old ground. So, work the new ground!

When you create a positive attitude, life becomes delectable. Trying to go back into the past or even stand still, is impossible – so give it up! Nature moves forward. Get in the flow of moving forward. Feel the *now*. It's immensely liberating.

When you liberate yourself in these ways the calming, natural flow of the 'heart' within you blossoms. This happens by degree. Sometimes we take two steps forward and one step back, and so on, but this accords with our tendency to let go in small steps rather than instantly.

Prosperity Consciousness

You may soon be experimenting with gaining access to your subtle energy, if you haven't done so already, based on information in this book and any other allied material you may be researching.

What you will doubtless discover is that the more you are able to easily acquire or change most of what you desire or need, the less emphasis you will put on desire. This may sound paradoxical but it comes about because you are changing your *perspective* concurrent with reducing your stress, suffering, problems etc. You are expanding your natural flow of creative, rather than analytical, thought.

At one time you may have thought that more cars, furnishings, money (and such material abundance) would be the answer to your prayers. Even if you use focused visualisation to build material wealth – a very basic type of acquisition technique – you will run out of steam when, with your unconditioned perspective, you realise that material stuff just comes and goes.

If you become able to easily acquire material substance by using your inner subtle energy, you will probably have become quite integrated and 'refined' in your thinking, so you are unlikely to project negativity through wealth.

By all means have as much material stuff in this life as you desire. There is absolutely nothing wrong with acquiring material wealth. We are in an economic world. Money buys things. The sale of goods brings employment and, therefore, much needed support to communities. Money is a positive energy unless it is hoarded pointlessly.

But material stuff is impermanent so it is not ultimately fulfilling. Temporary pleasure does not lead to lasting happiness. What virtually everyone is looking for is that something which is forever lasting and non-changing; preferably some sort of love.

The outer recognition of your progress in self-empowerment is that you will reach a level of perspective where your life will have become much more stable without many anxieties. You will in fact have reached a more fulfilled state, not because you have acquired more in a material sense but because your self-accountability has been acknowledged and accepted by you. You become more secure within yourself.

What happens, when you are reasonably integrated with your

higher self, is that you become aware that you are arriving nearer to the state you have always yearned for regardless of desires, material status, judgements, projections or anything else.

Thereby, if you then encounter further material gain you will treat it differently, probably more wisely, than when you thought that material gain was going to be the comfort that creates fulfilment.

Therefore, do not worry about material thoughts. They will not harm your unfoldment, as long as they are not destructive thoughts.

I have laboured the emphasis on this point because I have noticed a growing population of 'pseudo-spiritual' types, as well as countless social extremists, who portray, consciously or subconsciously, that riches are the root of unfairness – and that the rich are somehow harming the poor by creating an unfair world.

To my mind the only total fairness, in terms of wealth, could come about if everyone was wealthy and not if everyone was poor. This, however, is not likely to be achieved in the short term, if ever.

The story of Animal Farm depicts the result of attempts to produce 'fairness' in an everyone-has-the-same (but still needs leaders) society. The leaders of such regimes gain power while the vast majority, who the leaders were aiming to serve, lose their personal power and their freedom. Wealth is power. Self power for the maximum number of people doesn't debase anyone. The seized, misappropriated power of oppressive leaders over the general populace is what debases us.

The message in this book is about enhancing self power for all, not the few. Self power – control over your life – will produce the maximum happiness and fairness that can be hoped for on this planet. Individual prosperity should be encouraged, not suppressed. If it is stifled the masses will suffer exceeding unfairness at the hands of power freaks.

Gururaj recommended a useful tip regarding the attainment of wealth. Money is an enormous energy, so it flows just like any other energy. Find places to apportion your money, however little you may have at this moment. If you sit on money it will not grow, it will eventually stifle you. If you give out money it will come back to you in great multiples.

What flows out comes back to you. This is another universal law. You will have to accept the principle here that the flowing back to you could occur in this lifetime or in a future life. That will not go down too well with you if you are only concerned with this lifetime. If you are, you'll be restricting your evolutionary progress and your happiness.

The evolutionary principle here is that our quest for wealth as a cushion is futile, because such a quest is based upon preserving the status quo. We should be looking to free ourselves – because that is our nature – rather than hold on to anything.

I am not referring to business here. Business is constructive to the world provided that it doesn't bring about too much power (over others) for a few individuals. Most owners of businesses deserve what they earn. But trying to increase your wealth simply to build a money pile is fruitless.

It is better to look for opportunity. Provide for your basic needs first, of course. For instance if you are wealthy you could help somebody in real need, without any thought that they owe you anything – not even the money you give. Put money in charity boxes. Let money flow away from you without hanging on to it. Spend freely but sensibly. Someone else benefits when you spend. Waste is not to be encouraged.

To help with the idea of money flowing through you, rather than sticking to you, Gururaj even suggested throwing (a small amount) of money away in the street in the hope that someone deserving might pick it up!

The idea here is not to be irresponsible with money. The guiding rationale is that the more you free your mind, the more expansive you become, and the more of everything in the universe will flow through you.

Prosperity is not just about money or material wealth. Prosperity applies to all aspects of your life including happiness. Money is just one item in prosperity. You will be prosperous in happiness if you have a happy attitude. The same universal law – what flows out flows back – works with everything.

Likewise, poverty consciousness can affect you in the same way if you think, "I'm poor", all the time. You can surely grasp by now that if you are destitute in terms of either money or happiness, or anything else, your thinking process, based on the principles described earlier in this book, albeit subconscious, has brought on the circumstances.

You will doubtless recognise that the guiding axiom of letting energy flow has been considerably examined elsewhere in this book. It is such an important foundation to improving the circumstances of your life.

To reinforce your determination to let everything flow, do keep in mind that an irrefutable fundamental of unconditioning is that you accept the dictum of change being necessary and then set about changing *yourself*.

To close out on this subject I would again emphasise the need to permanently keep one eye on your whole evolution. Yes, this is another axiom I am accentuating! Your attitude to your unfoldment can affect your future lifetimes in either a positive or a negative manner.

Prosperity in all areas of life – not just material wealth – can be developed by having an open, non-attached attitude. If you become non-judgemental regarding things outside you, you should be able to accelerate the process of integration with your higher self. Consequently a greater abundance of everything positive will flow through you.

You can also slip down the prosperity scale if you are not vigilant. In particular, if you are wealthy this lifetime you are not likely to know whether you have earned this privilege in previous lives or you have acquired wealth as a test for yourself. This is an important point to consider because wealth is definitely a test for people.

The test is to find out if you can handle wealth and use it as a positive energy – to further advance your evolution.

Wealth can be a positive energy or a negative energy, dependent upon how it is handled. It is so easy to become either complacent or closed (or "tight") once your purchasing power is superior to that of the majority of society. If you tighten your hold on money – done because you use it as a self-protective device – you will implode your evolution which means establishing a less joyous position again for yourself at some future point rather than establishing a more joyous one.

Self-Love

During my decades of teaching subtle-mind techniques I asked almost every one of my students, "Do you love yourself?" Most of them answered in the following way, "I love my partner and my children. I try to love others. By loving me do you mean do I *like* myself?"

This response comes about because the question is not properly understood. It is not understood because the (limited) mind thinks of humans as objects rather than multi-dimensional consciousness.

Like this, loving yourself or other people is usually measured on a scale of adoration or of need, admiration etc. However, as we have discussed, love is not personal attachment. Love is the source that supports everything. Love is the true wholeness of life.

Therefore, love for yourself is initially the acknowledgement, the acceptance, of what we are.

In appreciating the wholeness of what you are, you respect yourself. You cease to deny your whole reality. Consequently, you open yourself up to the greater you that is the free, unencumbered, endless-potential you who is flowing with nature in the sphere of all possibilities.

So loving yourself does not expand your ego in a boastful or preservative way. And it doesn't deny others any love that may flow through you. Loving yourself comes to the fore as you unfold yourself. It is part and parcel of affirming that you are responsible for yourself; accepting that no-one else is ultimately responsible for you or the circumstances in which you find yourself.

In loving yourself truly and fully you *become* love. This is the greatest objective you can achieve. When you become love you are unrestricted. As well as benefiting yourself, the people around you and even the environment benefit from the energy that flows through you.

So, if you are not yet aspiring to self-love, it is not that you hate yourself. It is that you deny yourself. Denying yourself is done unintentionally, when you don't acknowledge what your Self actually is, which means you are denying yourself your SELF. The Real Self is the real you that is present all the time. When you don't acknowledge your Real Self you are trying to avoid your Real Self, whether you know this or not.

Much benefit ensues in your life once you recognise this denial in yourself. Then you start wanting to turn the situation around.

Typically, denial is expressed in forms of emotional escapism, which attempt to form a barrier to uncovering yourself. You can discover this when you are 'facing yourself', as described in an earlier chapter.

A few behavioural examples of this type of denial are:
- keeping feelings and fears unexpressed;
- being closed rather than open; being judgemental or blaming or criticising others;
- talking profusely to the point of boring others;
- becoming paranoid;
- being prudish or assuming yourself to be above others;
- filling in every moment with trivia or noise so as to avoid silence;
- needing to control, excessively
- avoiding serenity

(List your own traits – as many as you can imagine – when you are practising the process of uncovering yourself.)

Traits such as these, which apply to all of us, exemplify the barrier to self love we've unwittingly built. These resistances are attempts to stop evolution, prevent change and preserve the status quo. But there is no stopping the move forward of evolution, so these endeavours are pointless as well as harmful to your health and your longevity potential. Nothing can stop the eternal reaction and replication of energies which pushes the universe on through change after change, including your evolution. It's an unchallengeable law.

So, facing up to inevitable change is also a process of loving yourself. If you get into the flow of change – jumping on to the unstoppable juggernaut of nature – you will release yourself from so many burdens and discover unbounded joy.

Being honest about your fears and feelings is a good way to start unravelling all these (real) self-denials. If you start dealing with your fears and feelings you will almost literally melt an ice block. You release so much of the real you because the whole process of maintaining mental barriers, based on locking feelings inside you, is like an ice block requiring as much of your energy as any other deep freeze appliance.

Even the fear of death can be overcome if you are honest with yourself. You can make a start, in this respect, by admitting that you are fearful of the unknown.

Many people say they do not fear death while they admit they fear some of the other things in life. That is because they don't want to confront the things they fear in life (even simple things like hurting a relative's or a friend's feelings) and they would rather be dead than go through the process of overcoming the fear.

If you are one of these people you will find, by studying yourself truly, that you are trying to protect yourself by hiding what you really feel. Get over it! These self-protection attempts are self denial and they stilt your evolution, causing you pain during embodied life.

Escapist tendencies usually stem from childhood experiences. It is completely understandable that children sometimes protect the one who harms them, particularly if this is a relative. However, it is up to you, if you have suffered in this way, in childhood or adulthood, to get the burden unloaded. This is part of the test you have given yourself this lifetime.

When you *love* yourself you will move yourself on to better, freer evolution, despite your connection to any other person on this planet. Personal connections are temporary and they always contain tests and opportunities to *grow*.

Self denial is *joy* denial. Why continue all this suffering when there is a pain-free existence running alongside you on parallel tracks, and all you have to do is step aboard?

Love yourself!

Self-Being

Self-being is the second aspect of *being* the real you. The first aspect is the process of loving yourself, as discussed in the latter paragraphs, by which you gain self-freedom and expansiveness.

This second aspect concerns accepting yourself, in a relaxed yet positive manner. You need to get away from either putting on a false front for others to see or from trying to be like someone else.

There is no need to copy other people in this life or to present to the world anything other than who you are. You are perfect.

There is no imperfection in the universe and there is no imperfection in your part of the whole evolutionary picture. Everything is happening with perfect precision. Your body and the way your mind is acting right now is not an accident.

For sure, you should put a lot of energy into life and try to improve your thinking process, your happiness quotient and your circumstances. But *acceptance* of what you are is a vital key to moving forward in an improved condition.

You can't bring yourself all the benefits I've written about if you don't move away from your fears. And you won't move away from your fears if you continue with a false façade, which is sometimes used in an attempt to fool yourself and everyone else that things are *other* than they really are.

To admirers of Christ, Gururaj would say, "Don't try to be the same as Jesus. You will only achieve being a second class Jesus. Why not become a *first class you*, because that is who you are right now? You will reach the highest heights of consciousness, just like Jesus did, and all those other Masters, by unfolding your evolution in the way that it happens to you and not like it happened for someone else. We all have a different story, a different route."

So, accept your body and your abilities and your upbringing as being the perfect condition for you. Accordingly, you can make your path of self improvement a light and easy affair because you are not hiding in a false you. Make yourself a fantastic you. It is simple to be loved and to be happy. However, it is only simple if you act as yourself.

People will love you for being yourself. There is no doubt of that. Everyone can see if you portray any falsities, so you are not fooling anybody if you are not being yourself. You will not be loved so much if you keep up fake appearances.

Just be yourself. Admit your weaknesses and strive to overcome those weaknesses that are surmountable. Life will be simpler, more enjoyable and rewarding. You will also gain confidence *and* achieve your goals more easily.

The basis of portraying a false facade or filling every moment with trivia (etc.) stems, once again, from attachment to the little self and a failure to prioritise the Real Self. This is a major stumbling block caused by the mind insisting that everything around us is separate and not conjoined. In this way the mind insists that you suffer from events of the past or projections of the future.

If you think about uncovering yourself in respect of your traits, which is a vital factor in becoming non-attached, you cannot leave out the purpose of your life. Nor can you leave out the purpose of your life in any of the other unconditioning and unfolding matters I have talked about. So we see all aspects of the subject matter, particularly unconditioning, merging into each other.

If you can discover your purpose for this life you have taken on, a whole new vista of existence, in your mind, emerges. This is very freeing and fulfilling.

Have you ever read the very popular little book The Why Am I Here Café? This book highlights for you that if you don't know why you came here you really have missed the point. John Strelecky, the author, puts this over in such a way that you cannot deny that everyone needs to address this subject. What is also very convincing is that by addressing the matter you gradually resolve it. This undoubtedly results in living a happier and more fulfilled life.

Non-Separation

Most of us have great difficulty, at first accession, acclimatising to the idea of everything in existence being connected, as a oneness.

If we revert to the story of Wunspot, the allegory at the beginning of this book, we can see that any limitation of consciousness is self-imposed because of the comfort zones into which we settle. These comfort zones shape themselves around what we think we can cope with, based on three-dimensional stuff.

Trying to imagine what one-ness is actually like is a prime example of how our thought limitations keep us in confusion. When we form a projection of everything being connected together we can't stop thinking of objects and spaces.

When you are appropriately aligned and attuned, you will be living 'in the moment' and not prioritising memory of the past or projection of the future. You will thereby automatically reveal to yourself (that you have known all along) that you are a unity and not an individual boxed-in human mind. In that knowingness you (re)cognize too that everything in existence outside of unity-ness is 'mind'.

Re-cognition comes about by degree from the moment you start using practices such as meditation and other unfoldment tools, which all reduce the intensity of your mind's self-denigration tendency.

When you truly live in the moment your self-empowerment becomes supreme. Everything is in this moment anyway, whether you know it or not; good health and bad health; riches and poverty, judgment and discrimination; love and fear. When you truly live this moment the power to choose becomes yours – to move from any set of conditions to another set of conditions.

After you start to meditate regularly you will soon just stop in some moment in normal activity, thinking, "Ah, I know something here, something is just right, something is recognised," without knowing exactly or concretising what has happened. The more you continue with unconditioning the more realisation, that actuality is a unity, comes about.

The full appreciation of the universal mind can become apparent to you while you are embodied on this Earth, but this is not essential for improving this life or future lives for yourself.

For most people, a gradual awakening is preferred. There are various exercises you can do during normal waking hours that help you move smoothly into the appreciation of non-separation. I will mention just two of them here.

The first of the two is a mental exercise, related to prioritising two words in your daily life. These two words are NOWHERE and NOTHING. What you do with these words is split them in two. Nowhere becomes Now-Here and Nothing becomes No-Thing. The link between the two original words and the split words remains.

Now-Here is a reminder as well as an affirmation. We are living in the NOW. There is actually no past and no future because time, as we perceive in it in the three-dimensional state, does not exist.

Everything that has ever happened or ever will happen is happening NOW. This is not a theory. Science has acknowledged it. Therefore there is no point in building up too much anxiety about circumstances in this world. Just go with the flow and live the now.

'Nowhere' is a reminder to help us dispense with the idea that space, which, like time, does not really exist. Where are we? Now and here – Nowhere. It is only our restricted thinking process that convinces us we are somewhere.

By all means try the simple practice in the Appendices. I call it I Am Now. I use it every day.

No-Thing is a similar reminder and another useful affirmation. Thing means material object. But, in reality, there is no time or space so there is no thing. Our three dimension based perception insists that separate pieces of solid matter are the basis of life. This is such folly because this misconception causes all our suffering.

Some people are fearful of the No-Thing concept. This is because they are extremely attached and don't want to accede to the idea that "I am nothing".

The way to overcome such fear is to get used to the idea that when you give up the concept that "I am something" you actually gain something; you don't lose anything.

You are not going to lose your identity by introducing higher and less restricted consciousness. Whether you are in this body or beyond this life you are going to gain identity.

Think of Wunspot and Tooway (chapter 1) emerging into less restricted consciousness. They don't lose anything, they gain. By accepting higher dimensions you are going to *add on* to your present identity far more joy, freedom, confidence, competence and knowledge, which lead to self-direction of your destiny, instead of the buffeting around you receive from relative non-knowledge in restricted consciousness (which you have bestowed upon yourself).

The second of the two exercises is the 'self-recognition' practice whereby you can discover that you lose nothing of yourself by surrendering your little tangled-up self to your inner higher consciousness.

I have taught both newcomers and experienced meditators this exercise to good effect. It is not meditation as such. It is a practical experience of learning to be at one with yourself. It can help to release many fears including the fear of letting go of your ego or relinquishing your bullet-proof defence mechanism.

The very simple self-recognition exercise is described in the Appendices. It can be particularly helpful if you have a problem being alone with yourself or knowing yourself deeply.

These little self-discovery measures, if you need them, are just the start of what you can do for yourself in terms of coming to the realisation that we are not separate beings. As you become adept at meditation and contemplation you will ease into joyful acceptance of what you are and what you are not.

Everything you perceive is thought. Every little thing you see in front of you right now is nothing but thought created by the impression of separation. But the solid and the spiritual are not separate. It is only the limited angle from which you view it all that perpetuates your idea that reality is solid.

Wholeness is unlimitedness. When wholeness – your actuality – dawns on you, you are beyond all separation. In that state of consciousness there is no thought of limiting your Self into separate parts.

In reaching the state of Self-Realisation you will have gone beyond the opposites. The opposites are what *justify* the universal existence, such as light and dark, heat and cold, negative and positive – all the opposites, which exist in everything.

In the perfectly balanced (mind) state, you are in the centre of yourself. There are no opposites any more. There is only one thought. There is no separation. And the only remaining thought is not thought as such because it is beyond thought. In one-ness there is no process of thinking. It just IS.

Non-separation is the Way Forward

There could be several different reasons why you could have indulged in this book or books of a similar vogue.

You could be seeking knowledge of what you really are or why you're here on this planet, moving beyond what convention has to offer. Convention, after all, is based on the consensus of the masses and the masses do not have the answer to life. The masses base their reality on images.

You could be trying to infuse relaxation into your life. Both meditation and knowledge of your actuality, once accepted, help you in this regard. Stress is a killer but it can be overcome if you understand yourself properly and take up the necessary antidotes to stress.

You could be interested in what happens after death, either from curiosity or from fear that you want to overcome.

You might consider you have suffered unduly in this life and want to know the reason and the way forward.

You could have simply been curious as to how to improve your lot in this life, even though your interest could initially be in magnetising to yourself material stuff or love.

I have emphasised that nothing can be achieved without determination or without change. Persistence cannot fail you but lethargy or laziness can. You can take all the self-help courses in the world but if you put nothing in you get nothing out.

You cannot fail at anything if you have persistence. If something doesn't work out, dust yourself off, as the saying goes, and start over. This is part of life. Bad experiences happen to everybody. They are not failures. They are the education that you're here on this earth to receive. The more that is learned, in respect of your existence, the better life becomes.

Every problem in life stems from our sense of separation. If you can only glimpse One-ness – just once – you will know there is no death and there is no birth; there is no journey at all. It is only mind that creates all the images.

So, the experience of non-separation is the key to life because, if you remove the illusion of separation, you remove all fears and all problems.

Seeking stillness and living in the now as much as possible will help you to start knowing who you really are. Cutting out mind stuff, if only for very short periods (for a start), brings results by appreciating what non-separation really means. As consciousness expands, appreciation of wholeness increases.

An individual's appreciation of non-separation grows gradually, like a flower slowly opening up, when using correctly applied meditation techniques followed up with the unconditioning principles outlined.

Affirmations

Affirmations use the conscious mind as a reverse process…
Creating a deep impression upon the subconscious, of something positive, you will automatically eradicate that which is negative

– Gururaj

Finally, let's address the benefits to be gained by using affirmations.

As you have read, everything stems from thought. The thought process directs your life. The engine of thought is your brain. If you work your brain in a positive way, your thoughts will bring to you whatever you want. The more integrated you are with your higher (inner) self, the better this will work.

Affirmations are positive thoughts as well as definitive commitments.

Affirmations have more impact by using the "I *am*" stance, rather than the "I *will be*" stance. An affirmation confirms something. The mind helps you issue the instruction but the subtle self picks up on whatever you want because everything is here and now. The mind can think about a future because it lives in time and space but, as I've said, in actuality the whole of eternity is in this moment. Therefore when the subtle mind is predominant you 'pick up' on things efficiently. The ordinary mind works on past and future which is not real so it has little real power in comparison.

In simple form, let's say a mathematician wants to become a master at his (or her) skills. The mathematician can affirm "I am a master mathematician". If this affirmation process continues the mathematician will become a master. This comes about because the person is not planning to stop at degree level or become an ordinary teacher or employee but is totally determined to get to the very top in his subject. But if he'd tried to affirm, "I *will* become a master mathematician", there is an obstruction built in to the affirmation – so it will not have worked.

Thereby this person would go on and on absorbing maths, practising maths, probably becoming a renowned professor, because there was no indecision. "I am a master mathematician" is an absolutely positive affirmation and, if continued endlessly, would lead to the goal. Only over-doubting or losing positive conviction or getting bored with maths – any of the negatives – could cause the mathematician to fall short of the goal.

Thoughts are words said silently. However, thoughts are often interrupted by other thoughts and therefore fragmentation takes place, as we have seen. Words said aloud are very useful, as affirmations, because the sound reverberates and their repetition can be very one-pointed. One-pointedness is the key to achievement. Therefore affirmations should be spoken aloud.

Now, how can affirmations help you in respect of anything you have read about in this book?

Let's take the example of your desire to become less negative, if that applies to you. You could simply affirm "I am positive", or, even more specifically, "Every day, in every way, I am positive. I am always positive."

Be very specific and don't use negative words. The subtle mind doesn't understand negative words like 'not'. So, you can't use "I am not fearful". You have to use "I am fearless".

A writer who wanted to become a much better writer could affirm, "I am an extremely competent writer. I write everything perfectly. I am the best writer. My writing is outstandingly good." And so on.

Affirmations work better if you do them just after you have meditated for at least 15 minutes. Then the logical mind is subdued, the creative mind is more open and you are aligned with your subtle energy, which will take the energy of the affirmation to a very deep level.

After you have repeated your affirmation 10 or 20 times, which is sufficient, with 10 seconds or greater interval between each repetition, be silent for a minute or two and possibly finish off your session with a few very slow deep breaths. Deep breathing also imbibes subtle energy. You can learn deep breathing techniques for best results.

Beyond practical things, you may also want to use affirmations to help your spiritual unfoldment. You can use whatever phrases you wish. Often used are, "I am love", "I am one", "I am the universal self", or "I am existence itself". Once again this is better done at meditation time.

Here are a few more possible examples. These can be

rearranged or replaced ad lib – words in brackets are for guidance, not for saying aloud:

- I am multi-dimensional (not just 2, 3 or 4 dimensional)
- All dimensions are consciousness (not matter)
- Consciousness is controlled by me
- Whatever I focus upon is the limitation I insist upon (hence my containment in this apparent solid state)
- I am the vibrational (4th) dimension as well as the solid one
- I am the subtle (5th) dimension that overcomes time and space
- I am the highest dimension in duality – the ultimate bliss
- I am one – the one that is all and knows no other
- I am existence, knowledge, bliss – here and now

You can also read affirmative material from great teachers. Reference to outstanding figures who have, or had, determination and knowledge can help you unfold the truth and strength within you. Much religious reference and ritual is so based. As I have said, it is good for one-pointedness of intention.

An option below, to assist you, is an affirmative (extract from a) talk by one of my favourite teachers, Swami Vivekananda. This particular extract inspired me to move on as far as possible with self-realisation. So I will share it with you – at the conclusion of this subject and at the conclusion of this book.

Do read more of this stuff. When we face truth it often stings, possibly because we are feeling temporarily content with our little lives, ignoring our position of self responsibility for our evolution but also missing out on inherent self power this lifetime. But truth is what solves all problems as well as all mystery and brings us to a position of great joy and control over our destiny.

One truth is that you cannot keep the circumstances you are in now for very long, however hard you may try. So, it's worth doing something towards getting in the flow of evolution rather than being complacent. Complacency leads to an unresolved or wasted life.

From: Vedanta Voice of Freedom – extracts from Swami Vivekananda's talks
(Available from Ramakrishna Vedanta Centres throughout the world)

'THE OPEN SECRET'

None can die. None can be degraded forever. Life is but a playground, however gross the play may be. We may receive blows but, however knocked about we may be, the Soul is there and is never injured. We are that Infinite.

Thus sang a Vedantist: "I never had fear or doubt. Death never came to me. I never had a father or mother, for I was never born. Where are my foes? – for I am All. I am Existence, Knowledge, Bliss Absolute. I am It. I am It. Anger and lust and jealousy, evil thoughts and all these things never came to me, for I am Existence, Knowledge, Bliss Absolute. I am It. I am It."

That is the remedy for all disease, the nectar that cures death. Here we are in this world, and our nature rebels against it. But let us repeat: "I am It. I am It. I have no fear or doubt or death. I have no sex or creed or color. What creed can I have? What sect is there to which I should belong? What sect can hold me? I am in every sect."

However much the body rebels; however much the mind rebels, in the midst of uttermost darkness, in the midst of agonizing tortures, in uttermost despair, repeat this once, twice, thrice, evermore. Light comes gently, slowly, but surely it comes.

Many times I have been in the jaws of death, starving, footsore, and weary. For days and days I had no food, and often could walk no farther. I would sink down under a tree, and life would seem to be ebbing away. I could not speak. I could scarcely think. But at last the mind reverted to the idea: "I have no fear or death. I never hunger or thirst. I am It! I am It! The whole of nature cannot crush me – it is my servant.

"Assert thy strength thou Lord of lords and God of gods! Regain thy lost empire! Arise and walk and stop not!"

Thus, however darkness comes, assert this reality and everything adverse must vanish. For, after all, it is but a dream. Assert yourself again and again, and light must come.

You may pray to everyone that was ever born, but who will come to help you?.. Help thyself by thyself. None else can help thee, friend. For thou alone art thy greatest enemy; thou alone art thy greatest friend.

Get hold of the Self, then. Stand up.

Don't be afraid. In the midst of all miseries and all weakness let the Self come out, faint and imperceptible though it be at first. You will gain courage, and at last like a lion you will roar out: "I am It! I am It! I am neither a man nor a woman nor a god nor a demon, no, nor any of the animals, plants, or trees. I am neither poor nor rich, neither learned nor ignorant. All these things are very little compared with what I am, for I am It! I am It! Behold the sun and the moon and the stars. I am the light that is shining in them! I am the beauty of the fire! I am the power of the universe! For I am It! I am It!

My real pleasure was never in earthly things – in husband, wife, children, and other things. For I am like the infinite blue sky; clouds of many colours pass over it and play for a second; they move off, and there is the same unchangeable blue.

Happiness and misery, good and evil, may envelop me for a moment, veiling the self, but I am still there. They pass away because they are changeable. I shine because I am unchangeable. If misery comes, I know it is finite; therefore it must die. If evil comes, I know it is finite. It must go. I alone am infinite, untouched by anything. For I am the infinite, that eternal, changeless Self.

Let us drink of this cup, this cup that leads to everything that is immortal, everything that is unchangeable. Fear not; believe not that we are evil or weak or small, finite, that we can ever die. It is not true.

This is to be heard of, then to be thought about, to be meditated upon. When the hands work the mind should repeat,

"I am it, I am it." Think of it, dream of it, until it becomes the bone of your bones, the flesh of your flesh, until all the hideous dreams of littleness, of weakness, of misery and of evil have entirely vanished and no more then can the Truth be hidden from you, even for a moment.

– Swami Vivekananda (1863 – 1902)

Epilogue

The process of unfolding the inner consciousness, for incomparable fulfilment as well as self-empowerment, must start with the mind itself.

Can you imagine how free you would feel if you were unbelievably self-empowered and unencumbered from fear? Thousands of your fellow human beings can testify that this point can be reached, in this lifetime. In this liberated state you know, rather than project, because you become integrated with your subtle Self. Then everything changes. Everything comes to you. You allow yourself to grasp everything in the universe and everything in the universal mind without even having to reach out. The joy and feeling of freedom this state of unfoldment brings is indescribable.

The inherent remedy that accompanies integration, the remedy to the confusion of not fully understanding the meaning of life, is brought about by simply daring to go beyond the mind.

Using the mind as a tool, rather than allowing it to be a dictator, is the shortest and the only solution. The incredibly simple subtle mind techniques to which I have referred are the foundation on which you can build liberation from limitation. And, once you try them, you'll immediately reveal to yourself that going beyond the mind is not a scary proposition but a beautiful one.

Consciously or unconsciously, each of us wants to be liberated. Each of us really wants to be free because freedom is our nature. We want to be free from mental suffering, free from incompetence, free from poverty, free from physical threat, free from sadness and loneliness, free from the intolerability of thoughts of losing something or someone dear to us. We want to be liberated from the shackles that bind us.

Your liberation can start with a straightforward thought such as, "I am turning away from this eternal spiral of pointlessness and I am releasing myself from the bondage that builds incessant obstacles." Any such line of thought is all that is needed to step onto the path of self-strength and immutable happiness. These are effective thoughts too, because they don't threaten the ego, so the mind will be happy to keep them in view.

The eternal pure consciousness, which is the *real* self, is useable. It's flooding every single cell of your body, yet it remains veiled for the most part, because the cunning ego, which constantly provides illusory barriers and instructs the mind to seek answers to life from outside yourself.

It is an elementary process to learn techniques that will allow you to deal with thoughts so that you master your thoughts. The correct techniques don't threaten the ego, they coerce the ego into becoming less dense, allowing you to use the ego as your slave rather than be enslaved by it.

By using subtle mind techniques regularly, you turn the key to the door that previously barred your exit from the imprisonment of self-limitation.

In this way the shackles that bind you to your self-imposed sentence of suffering start to fall away. The goal you have always been seeking, knowingly or unknowingly, comes into view. You start to control your destiny – including shaping many of the happenings in what you have left of this lifetime.

Unfoldment can be a long and winding path but it need not be. It is not as if one has to grow a new self. The liberating consciousness that is sought is already fully developed, fully competent, within each of us. Parting the veils just needs a little determination.

On this last point, my first proof reader, Carole Sheppard, said something pertinent during our discussions. I therefore decided to add these final three paragraphs in hopes of emphasising the most important notion in this book, for clarification. Carole's comment, typical of most who read this kind of book for the first time, was that the *whole life* concept is extremely fascinating but it's a shame there's such a long way to go between where you are now and experiencing the eternal oneness.

My response is a reiteration. There is nowhere to go. There is no distance at all. There is no hill to climb. Everything is *here* and *now* in that beautiful one-ness. It is only the mind that refuses to let go of separate-ness and it does so because samskaras are like a heavy yoke on your shoulders, insisting that the ego predominates. Making up your mind, determinably, to switch from separate-ness to one-ness, is all that's required.

What you think is real is unreal. Let go of the unreal and you will solve your life and you will enjoy your evolution.

Glossary

Actuality – Pure Consciousness

Anhankara – the ego

Attunement – aligning with the natural inner self

Bliss – the highest experience of consciousness (where duality remains)

Brahman – the 'spirit' or eternal source energy

Buddhi – the intellect

Chitta – the memory

Dharma – a duty to oneself to take on self-accountability /self-responsibility

I – Pure Consciousness

IT – Pure Consciousness

Karma – a build up of personal energy imbalance which needs balancing out

Manas – the lower mind

Maya – attachment to what we perceive in the three-dimensional sphere

Mental Body – Images you project / perceptions you accept

One-ness – Pure Consciousness

Pure consciousness – the only wholeness actuality existent – it exists in everything

Real Self – Pure Consciousness

Samskaras – untraceable bundle of impressions causing one's life path

Shakti – accessible eternal subtle energy

Subtle Body – (after death) mental body infused with higher consciousness

Subtle Mind – your more efficient mind, less blocked, infused with higher consciousness

Uncondition – overcome thoughts that have caused barriers; retrain thinking / perception

Bibliography

UK satsangs (talks by Gururaj) referred to:
Numbers are library references:
Acceptance: 77–17; 77–19; 78–45; 79–2; 84–14
Affirmations: 77–4; 77–11; 77–14; 77–30; 78–11; 78–34; 79–11; 80–41B; 86–16
Angels: 76–6B; 77–19; 78–11; 78–66; 84–14
Attachment & Non-attachment: 76–2A; 76–8; 77–33; 77–35; 78–38; 79–5; 79–32; 79–39; 85–4; 85–11
Avatars: 76–5; 77–22; 77–33; 78–39; 78–61; 79–1; 80–07; 80–16; 81–13; 82–8
Awareness: 76–8; 77–6; 77–24; 77–31; 78–8; 78–57; 79–1; 80–22; 80–27; 80–41A; 81–5; 86–10
Be Yourself: 80–34; 80–38; 82–8; 84–8; 84–14; 85–20; 86–2
Change: 76–10; 76–12; 77–11; 78–8; 79–7; 79–22; 79–28; 79–31
Christ: 76–8; 76–12; 77–22; 82–8; 79–1; 79–4; 80–5; 80–16; 81–6; 82–8; 82–13; 83–11
Conscious Effort: 76–1; 77–11; 77–29; 80–4; 80–13; 80–17
Contemplation: 78–2; 78–4; 79–30; 80–19; 84–20; 86–9
Death & Afterlife: 76–8; 78–33; 79–29; 79–31; 80–36; 82–6; 82–14; 84–14
Ego: 76–3; 76–7; 77–17; 77–20; 77–35; 78–7; 78–15; 78–35; 78–49; 78–59; 79–5; 80–15
Existence: 77–10; 77–20; 77–30; 78–4; 78–54; 78–60; 81–10; 83–2; 83–3; 83–11
Expectation: 77–21; 78–20; 79–2; 80–37; 8041A; 85–21
Facing Yourself: 76–9; 76–11; 82–17; 78–30; 78–34; 82–17; 85–19
Fear: 76–8; 77–6; 77–17; 77–20; 78–46; 79–23; 80–37; 81–8; 82–4; 82–14
Free Will: 77–9; 78–58; 78–64; 81–2
God – Personal & Impersonal: 76–2A; 76–13; 77–19; 78–44; 79–1; 79–35; 79–41; 81–13; 82–3

Appendices

'Moment One' – the anti-inertia game
(See 'Inertia' – ref. Page 102)
First, affirm that you want to get active or out of your lethargic mood – even if you feel you can't be bothered. Next, affirm that at 'moment one' you will spring to your feet and do something. Then count down, out loud, "five, four, three, two, one", and as you say "one" get up and move. If you are already standing, change your position.

Immediately do something you have not been doing while you were feeling lethargic. This could be going for a walk or cleaning something or making tea – absolutely anything you choose. But make it a *physical activity you don't have to think about*.

Don't analyse yourself and don't talk to anyone else about what you are doing. Just do something. If it is a short activity like making tea, decide, while you're making it, what will be your next activity after you've drunk it. Make that next activity something that will take half an hour at least, longer if possible.

Use 'moment one' as often as you need.

Visualisation
(ref. page 122/123)
The mechanics of visualisation, in short form, are as follows:
You should approach visualisation with guardedness and not complacency.

You can visualise anything at all and bring it to fruition if you are focused enough. Therefore a visualisation practice is best done after a meditation that will both relax you and increase your ability to focus. You must visualise with intensity whatever it is you desire or wish to change.

Let us say you are a business person who wants a contract to be signed. You could visualise the person who you want to sign that contract in every detail, in their office, the clothes he or she is wearing and the pen they are holding, the colour of the ink etc. You could visualise every detail about the environment – having practised *awareness* this will be easier – where you are sitting and the signing taking place.

The more detail you get into the surer the result will be. It is your ability to visualise – without any other thoughts creeping in, which would fragment the visualising energy – that brings about results. Practicing awareness and using a focal gazing meditation technique can help to enhance your ability to visualize. Stilling techniques of some kind are essential for gaining results.

One's positive karmic balancing plan needs to be put in train and samskaric adjustment started in order for the visualisation technique to be seriously effective.

Every thought goes out in the subtler spheres and every thought-energy is propelled forth and gathers momentum. Something *happens* with that energy.

The more you practise visualisation the more proficient you will become. Results are not necessarily forthcoming immediately. Time is not a reality so timing cannot be definitive. You can however demand a time scale if you want to. Everything is possible.

The only condition is that, in accordance with nature's flow, *you must give to receive*. No energy produced is a one way door. You must put in something yourself. The effort involved and the concentration is one outpouring of energy in itself but this is only aligned to the receiving end of the energy tube and not to the giving end. You must also *offer* something.

All energy, every happening, is balanced and counter balanced, ad infinitum. Consequently, it's inadvisable to draw piles of stuff towards you or develop new qualities with the intention of ending up in seclusion, having gained some sort of self-comfort or self-satisfaction. If you try to do this, the energy you have gained would force you into some sort of action – not necessarily to your liking – because nothing in manifestation can remain still. Everything in existence, be it material or subtle, is balanced out in some way or another. You can't steer energy in one direction without a reaction.

If you don't visualise the action and the reaction – how the newly acquired energy or quality will be dissipated in a definite way – then action could happen in some direction not suitable for you, similar to the example I referred to in this book about the Rolls Royce. Many visualisation schools and methods of thought fail to point out this important point regarding reaction.

For the sake of simplicity, let us say you successfully visualise an amount of money. What would you do with it? It would be well to use it constructively and not just buy stuff for yourself. You could think of the scenario as a giving back for something received. Someone else who deserves help could then be getting help by means of your (positive) visualisation and actions.

So, beware of trying to become a rich recluse. If you happen to get through life with a pile of riches and you stop interacting, or you don't put anything back, you will surely pick up the counterbalance of that in a future life, if not this one.

For a fuller explanation, read the author's book New Life For Old – Guarantee to Make The Law of Attraction Work, an ebook currently being developed into a paperback.

I am now
(ref. page 154)

Have you ever tried confirming that there is only the present moment with which to concern yourself, by saying, "Now … now … now …" in times of mind turbulence? It's quite a stabilizer. Past and future cannot interrupt you if you seriously concentrate on this very moment. You might even want to do this, freely and frequently, for no other reason than bringing the reality of now-here into your life.

By repeating "now" insistently to yourself, you can cut out thoughts of past and future and *feel* a greater reality. Memories and projections are not a solution to anything. But living the now does bring about solutions. It's quite the opposite of what the mind thinks. What happens is that *now* brings forth the reality of "I am", as opposed to "I fear" or "I cannot solve". "I am" is one of the very few thoughts against which the mind cannot win a fight because it's a meaningful statement from the real you.

The Self-Recognition practice
(See Non-Separation – ref. Page 155)
This is like the first 'meditation' practice the author ever encountered

This incredibly straightforward, easy exercise is often looked at as too simplistic. However, there are three distinct potential benefits to be gained from it.

> The first benefit is in seeing yourself as separate to your mind, which will reinforce the idea that you are something natural, peaceful and real as opposed to a whirl of uncontrollable thoughts.
> The second is that you are going to automatically attest that the ego is not really you; that you need it but you can be advantaged by refining it.
> The third is that people who ordinarily find it difficult to be still and silent often discover, by doing this exercise, they can enjoy peace rather than be afraid of it.

Method: Take yourself to a quiet spot, preferably alone. By all means be accompanied if you feel anxious about this at first. Just sit as still as you can for one minute and then consciously jettison all the junk in your mind – meaning everything – to a place distant from you. Pick a specific place where you are throwing all the contents of your mind to. It could be a building or a rock face, up a tree – anywhere. To help you throw away all thoughts, you may be helped by imagining a trap door on your head opening and everything going up and out of your head (to the specified target area).

Just be as still as you are able, in your imaginary blank new self. Also be vaguely aware that the whole contents of your mind have gone off to the room or area that you chose to commit it to, but only for a few minutes. Be conscious that you are going to get your thoughts back whenever you want but for a few minutes you are going to relieve yourself of them. Your mind therefore will be quite happy to be taking a break. It has no fear because it knows you are going to need all the contents to come back very shortly.

You may not find pleasure in doing this at first. However, do keep it up because in time you will probably become comfortable with the whole exercise. Do it as often as you wish. The period of time can be anything you like, from a couple of minutes to about fifteen minutes.

If you are unsure at first, think about when you've been at the seashore staring at the tide lapping against the rocks. (If you've never done this try to imagine it or take yourself to a place of similar natural 'flow' and try it out).

When you start to stare at the rocks on the seashore you are witnessing the motion of nature. Because, at first, your mind is full of everyday intricacies you can often feel uncomfortable because the nature you are experiencing and your mind are at odds with each other. You can sometimes feel quite distressed for a while. But the longer you stay with the natural scene the more you get in touch with it. What happens after an hour or so is that you come to terms with the nature and your problems start to get into perspective; you feel better; you enjoy the experience.

The self-recognition exercise is meant to do much the same thing. You don't have to extend it for a long time period but if you can eventually get to a half-hour or more this would be good.

What you are doing is allowing the nature of *yourself* to be appreciated. The reason you feel good after communing with nature is that love, which is the energy you allow into your consciousness – and is your Real Self – makes you feel good. It lifts you up. It brings out the joyousness in you.

Nature is love. It is the flow, going on all the time, you more often than not resist. The nature of the sea shore (or other scene of nature) is the motion taking place. The nature of your inner self is peace and stillness. The love of somebody close to you is nature too. When you think loving thoughts that lift you up, you don't give your mind any space to interrupt your enjoyment, albeit the time period of your enjoyment might be very short.

What's emphasised here is 'flow'. By being still we get into the flow of our true nature. Although that flow may feel a bit alien at first, with continued practise it becomes a feeling of joy.

The more you do the practice, the more the joy of stillness will come to the fore. In the stillness a connection to everything existent is felt because, although you have lost the busy nature of the mind (which only *thinks* it has everything worked out), you have gained expansiveness and limitlessness to some degree. This gets blocked and produces barriers to nature when the machinations of your mind are predominant.

This little exercise is sometimes known as the 'throwing yourself away' practice. What it confirms is that if you mentally throw away everything inside you, you lose nothing. You acquire the knowledge that, by experiencing the stillness of yourself you are not going to disappear or be threatened in any way. You are going to gain – peace of mind, better health, solutions to your problems and so on. Many who have started doing this practice have gone on to thoroughly enjoy regular meditation, with all the attendant benefits, whereas they had previously been resistant to trying it due to being uncomfortable with silence and stillness.

A Profile of Gururaj Ananda Yogi (1932–1988)

Gururaj was born and raised Parsotam Narshi Bhana in India. He lived most of his life beyond age 20 in Cape Town, South Africa.

A brief synopsis of Gururaj's life up to age 44 is given below under 'chronology'.

Most pertinent to this profile is the period in Gururaj's life when he travelled extensively as a spiritual teacher. From the age of 44 until his demise, *which he predicted*, at age 56, he devoted himself to teaching groups of people, amounting to tens of thousands of students, the art of personalised meditation and life transforming yogas. His teaching continues in abundance through various channels in approximately 12 countries so far. The vast teaching – contained in thousands of pages of transcribed talks and various recordings – has continued after Gururaj's passing, because of the devotion of many of his chelas (close followers).

Paradoxically, the long term continuation of Gururaj's work will probably occur because of an outstanding event that surrounded his final months on Earth. As Gururaj said himself, his work may be relatively unnoticed for many decades or even centuries, after the present spate of enthusiastic activity to promote it, but then it will rise again, probably because of zeal and greed.

This is regrettable but this is the way mankind operates. Somebody in the future, Gururaj said, who has little or no connection with the true teachings given here during the 20th century, will form some sort of sect or religious organisation that will omit the basic message in the teaching, but glorify it in attractive ways in order to gain power, taking advantage of mass ignorance of truth. This is how many religions become established. In this case, Gururaj's glorification is likely to be built on the foundation of the main event that occurred, whether we like it or not.

What was this event? An astonishingly bright star was seen in the sky, the occurrence of which was a total amazement to astronomers, coinciding with Gururaj's 'last suppers' (as the event was referred to afterwards). Gururaj held a 10 day retreat – a 'spiritual holiday' – the only event of its kind ever held, in Cyprus during February 1987. Every supper was shared with all those gathered there with him. It was the only time Gururaj or any of those with him had ever been to Cyprus. The venue, in Limassol, was chosen randomly.

Gururaj was also sharing with his close ones a résumé of what he had taught because, he said, his demise was upcoming and he wanted to spend time with the chelas in a family farewell, ensuring that his followers were ready and able to continue his work. One of the facts he told the group was that he would not return to this planet again for 6,000 years.

He also spoke of a catastrophe that would occur, probably in the first half of the 21st century, if the people of this planet did not turn away from gross materiality to more spirituality. Remember this was in 1987, which was long before any of the international troubles, or the economic decline, starting in the decade beginning year 2000, were in view.

Everything discussed in Cyprus was recorded and the event included the inauguration of Guruaj's new title – Preatam.

During the interactive talks Gururaj was holding, on 24th February, the brightest stellar explosion of modern times – Super Nova SN1987A – appeared over Cyprus. The biblical connotations are obvious. Not surprisingly the occurrence was hailed by some as confirmation of the avatar status that had been rumoured about Gururaj for many years.

At various times, surrounded by some of his followers in total silence, Gururaj would enter the (highest) state of consciousness, known as Nirvikalpa Samadhi, for considerable periods of time. This is the highest state of consciousness a human being can attain. In this state of consciousness one gains the experience of the oneness of existence, which always has been existent and always will be. Very few humans can achieve this but it is well documented to have been achievable by Avatars. (Unrealised humans can glimpse the oneness state but cannot hold on to it because their mind is not sufficiently controllable.)

Thus the avatar status of Gururaj gained more and more credence. Even before he had given the first explanation of the Samahdi experience, in the 1970's, several people in his audiences stated that during the Samadhi sessions they had seen the face of Buddha, Jesus, Lao Tse and other renowned masters from the past. This continued on and off for several years.

Gururaj was a prolific poet. The following poem by him was not published until after his death and was not seen by most of his chelas while he was alive. This has also been lauded as a signal that the life of Gururaj was a reincarnation of (various, or one of the) great masters.

"I am your father, mother, friend, son and daughter
I am the creation buried deep down within you

Respond in which ever way you can ... for love I am
Give in whichever way you want, I will never command

You can demand anything from me for your needs; it shall be yours.
I will give it with a flower in my hand.

Seek you father, mother, daughter or son, lover or beloved –
You'll find only that in your mind's composed metre.

Pleasure or pain, avalanches, blizzard or rain,
The fragrance of the flower that I give will sustain you.

I have kept my promise. I have come again. "

It is not difficult to imagine, given the above detail, after Gururaj's passing in May 1988, there was a very strong interest in his work and quite a number of individuals were prepared to devote their time to continuing it. Consequently almost every word he spoke in over 1500 (unprepared) talks has been transcribed and much of this material has been published. Also continuing is the training of meditation using unique personally prescribed techniques established by Gururaj in the western world. This method is highly acclaimed throughout the world by hundreds of thousands of meditators. The number taught is expected to swell to millions in the near future.

Chronology
Gururaj Ananda Yogi was born on 3rd March 1932 as Parsotam Narshi Bhana in the province of Gujarat in India. As a child he displayed a remarkably advanced spiritual consciousness. At age 3, his questions were consistently about the meaning and purpose of life.

He wanted to experience the 'godhead' and at age 5 he ran away from home seeking to find it. He visited many temples and holy men. His frantic parents finally found him ragged and barefoot wandering through a village street. When questioned, he explained that he went to as many temples as possible, but that "the gods were lifeless and would not speak to me".

His life between the ages of 5 and 15 was in most respects quite normal for a child in his Indian culture. The one exception to this was his continuing overwhelming, intense desire to directly experience a reality far greater than his limited consciousness. This led him to the reading of many religious scriptures and books on philosophy.

His highly developed intuition made him more and more aware that what he sought actually lay within him, and within all human beings. He came across many names for this greater reality within. Some spoke of the Kingdom of Heaven Within, or the Divine Spark Within, while others spoke of the Universal Mind or the Real Self. The Western psychologist Carl Jung spoke of the Collective Unconscious and various Western philosophers spoke of the Superconscious Mind.

He knew that this area of Superconscious Awareness lay deeply buried beneath layers of conditioning in the subconscious mind. He intuitively sensed that if he could somehow penetrate these opaque strata of subconscious conditioning, the answers to all the anguished questionings of his conscious mind would be forthcoming.

His education and various encounters with gurus and wise sages told him that one of the classical methods for penetrating this greater reality was through meditation. But what kind of meditation? Practiced in what way and for how long? He could not answer these questions himself and he knew he required a teacher.

This raised yet another question – which teacher? There were many teachers professing to impart spiritual knowledge and practices in his native Indian culture. He knew that the teacher must be right for him, must truly possess the knowledge and the spiritual force to be able to lead him step by step on his inward journey towards the conscious experience of the Superconscious Self.

His search was rewarded when, in his late teens, after visiting many ashrams and gurus, in a monastery near Almora in the Himalayas he found the guru he had long sought – Swami Pavitrananda. Gururaj was led by him step by step through the illusory veils of the conditioned conscious and subconscious mind towards the Superconscious Self.

After a period of intensive and careful preparation under the direction of Pavitrananda, Gururaj reached the critical point in his development where he was ready for the breakthrough into full illumination. Gururaj stated that "for some time my meditations had been very deep and I knew that I was ready for the experience of Nirvikalpa Samadhi".

[Nirvikalpa Samadhi: The state of consciousness in which there is a permanent, fully opened channel between the conscious and superconscious mind].

Then on a hot afternoon the long-awaited experience arrived. In Gururaj's own words, "Pavitrananda casually summoned me to meditate with him. In Pavitrananda's presence I slipped almost immediately into a profound meditation. I merged into a state of blissful consciousness far beyond the realms of space and time."

He described it as a state of "joyful, eternal freedom, of immense peacefulness and yet vast power, transcending all the limitations and conditionings of my mind". He knew with certainty, beyond the possibility of description, that "what I was experiencing was in fact my Real Self". It was totally clear, he said, that "my mind, my body, my personality were only reflections and expressions of this real and true Nature."

Gururaj said, "When I surfaced from meditation two hours had gone by – but it could have been two minutes, so far had I been from ordinary time. When I opened my eyes, everything around me was covered in gold."

He could perceive with total, immediate certainty, not as a mental concept but as a living experience, that "everything around me – myself included – as simply dancing, vibrating patterns of energy. I just knew that I was the very same joyous, unbounded energy as everything and everyone around me – indeed of all of creation."

It was as if "my consciousness was their consciousness and their consciousness was mine," he said. At the same time it was "as if we were all part of a vast, infinitely larger consciousness." He also stated, "No words could even begin to describe the full reality of that experience – one must just have the experience to know."

[This state of illumined consciousness has been called by

many names. A Christian or Jew might speak of God-realisation, of reunion with their Divine Source. A Burmese Buddhist might speak of Nirvana, a Japanese Zen Buddhist of Satori or Enlightenment. The Western philosopher might speak of Unity Consciousness, an Indian philosopher of Brahman Consciousness. A Western psychologist might speak of Transpersonal Awareness. Perhaps the most neutral term used is Self-Realisation, since it does not imply any special religious or philosophical commitments.]

Having once fully and permanently entered the self-realised state, Gururaj could perceive with perfect clarity and simplicity a truth which he had often encountered in his philosophical reading. In his own words, "It was so very obvious to me that having realised this state, it made little difference how one arrived there – provided the path a person chose was right for that individual. One could be a Christian or a Jew, a Hindu or a Moslem, a Buddhist or a Taoist, a student of Eastern or Western philosophy."

Indeed, according to Gururaj, a person might follow a path without any of the usual religious or spiritual connotations. Perhaps they might be involved in a system of Western transpersonal psychology, such as that of Carl Jung's. Or they might be a practical person, immersed in the responsibilities of daily life, with very little time or concern for religious, philosophical or psychological theories. For this, according to Gururaj, was "a matter of direct personal experience – not of beliefs, philosophies or lifestyles".

According to Gururaj, what was of crucial importance was a sincere striving to reach beyond the limits of the petty ego, the small conditioned mind, to a larger reality. Whatever the path, one must follow it with real commitment and sincerity. If the sincerity and depth of commitment were there, then it was obvious to Gururaj from his own experience with Pavitrananda that a programme of proper meditation and self-help could also be of immense use, even invaluable.

Many such understandings and realisations emerged as the immediate aftermath of the youth's enlightenment experience.

But most important to him was the constant, deeply joyful fulfillment of a fully realised consciousness; he felt that there was absolutely nothing the world could offer him that would bring greater happiness or satisfaction than he already possessed. As a result, he began to entertain the idea of living a peaceful, reclusive life as a monk in some secluded Himalayan cave. However, it was not to be so.

Pavitrananda insisted that Gururaj immerse himself in the world. He was to become a householder and to thrust himself into the complex, dynamic, vital civilisation of the Western world. He was to know directly – by personal experience – the pleasures and pains, the joys and sorrows, the problems and solutions, the creativity and the fulfillment to be found in a full, active participation in the world. Having gained this practical experience, he could be far more useful to active, Western people when one day he would begin his work as a Spiritual Teacher. For it was his destiny to provide instruction and guidance – through meditation and self-help programmes – to many people in the modern Western world.

So it was necessary that he should marry, raise a family, and live and work in the West. In order to prepare himself for these responsibilities, he studied English and the practical subjects of commerce and accountancy. In his early 20s, having completed his studies, he sensed that the time was right for him to move to the West.

He emigrated from India to South Africa. The choice of South Africa was largely dictated by the ease of immigration as Gururaj and his father had lived in South Africa for three years when he was a child, which established his rights of residency.

Immersing Himself In Worldly Life

In South Africa Gururaj entered a business career. To pursue a successful career in the highly competitive modern business community inevitably requires much dedication, energy and creativity. In view of this, it must be understood that the Superconscious Mind is a virtually unlimited resource of energy and creative intuition. Having attained the self-realised state,

Gururaj had constant and far reaching access to this immense inner resource.

Consequently he possessed a phenomenal energy level and a highly developed intuitive mind. This intuition – a kind of creative "sixth sense" – would guide him with an almost unerring accuracy in making the immense number of practical, daily decisions that modern business demands. His energy was such that he required only 2 or 3 hours of sleep per night. This enabled him to work 14–16 hours per day and still fulfill his many other responsibilities and interests.

With such inner resources of creativity and energy, it was inevitable that he was very successful in his business career. Within a remarkably short-time he became the director of a number of companies.

It was always clear to Gururaj that the accumulation of wealth should never be the ultimate purpose of one's business activities. In his own words, "Wealth is not an end in itself. Money is simply a resource, such as any other man-made resource. The test of any resource is how well we use it. The real question is – do we use our collective or personal wealth in such a way as to uplift ourselves, or friends, families, or our communities? Is our wealth put to positive and creative use? Or, is it used only for personal comfort, pleasure, prestige, power etc – in others words to strengthen the small, limited ego?"

In accordance with this principle, Gururaj always used a sizeable portion of his business earnings – and much of his personal time – to further various spiritual or community projects. He was a major contributor in terms of time, energy and money to the founding of an Indian cultural society in Cape Town, South Africa – a major accomplishment for the Indian community there.

Business and community projects did not occupy all of his time or seemingly endless fund of energy for he married and raised a family. To anyone who came to know Gururaj well, it was evident that he had a deep and sincere devotion to his family. In spite of an extremely full schedule of activities and responsibilities, he always gave much time and love to the care and upbringing of his children. He had warmth and an intuitive way with children that was quite magical to witness.

Gururaj's ability to relate to children indicates a certain highly sensitive aspect of his personality. The outward, creative expression of this sensitivity (combined with the full access to the Superconscious) is found in yet another dimension of this multidimensional man – for Gururaj was a remarkably gifted poet.

Gururaj used poetry as an expressive medium for his inner realisations. He began writing poetry in his early adolescence, and had already received several awards in India by the age of 20. In fact, critics have favourably compared his work with Tagore's.

One of his beautiful poems, STILLNESS OF ETERNITY, is included here. This poem – as with all of his poetry – was written quickly and spontaneously, as if it flowed directly from the Superconscious Self to his pen, entirely bypassing the analytical intelligence of the conscious mind.

Winged birds of time fly on,
Flying to the rising sun and turning back at dusk:
A long journey it seems to reach back at starting point –
Winged birds, time's creatures, fly on

I, that am, forever still, know -
Of no journey's start, nor end, nor flight.

Your outspanning wings, measuring the sky,
Swift and slow, slow and swift,
Smiling at the wingless snail treasuring earth;
Both, in smog or dirt, in motion bound

I, that am, forever still, know –
Of no measure, nor motion, neither doing's undoing.

Bewildered you in your wingedness, the wingless too –
Chained by grooves of motion's air and earth -

Tossed and twirled and set afire, seemingly so new:
To fly on, to plod on, through many a life and birth

I, that am, forever still, know –
Of no air, nor earth, nor life nor birth, still ever new

By ordinary standards, to be a poet, a musician, a successful businessman, a community leader and a devoted family man would constitute a full life. It was certainly the fulfillment of Pavitrananda's injunctions to "immerse himself in the world". But it must be remembered that Pavitrananda's instructions to Gururaj were for a purpose. His active life in the Western world was to prepare him well for a time when, as a Spiritual Teacher, he would help guide other active, Western people toward self-realisation.

Service To Humanity
This, said Gururaj, "had been in the back of my mind all of those years, ever since my meeting with Pavitrananda."

Over the years, Gururaj became increasingly impressed with the central importance of meditation as a means of gradually acquiring access to the Superconscious Self. It also became clear that each person is a unique individual. Therefore in order to be fully effective, the meditation practice given to each person must be right for him as an individual. It must fit into one's individual life style as a whole, enhancing every area of life, work, marriage, personal relationships, etc., in the path one has chosen.

He evolved a method of selecting meditation practices that would meet the unique mental, physical, emotional and spiritual needs of each person. This method is based on ancient tradition, adapted for the ordinary householder who is seeking to improve their life in practical ways by utilising subtle energy from finer dimensions. Advanced practices are included for those who wish to deepen their experience and/or become much more integrated with the Self.

In 1975 Gururaj completed the business phase of his life. He continued to live in Capetown with his family, and took the vow of full-time service to humanity. The remainder of his life was devoted to helping people throughout the world in their spiritual quests for self-realisation.

To this end, Gururaj, together with other like-minded people in several countries, founded the International Foundation for Spiritual Unfoldment. Within just one year, individuals in nine different countries started national branches of the International Foundation for Spiritual Unfoldment (IFSU) to help make such meditation practices easily available to all individuals who might desire them.

There is an important point regarding Gururaj and his life and work which must be made very clear. According to Gururaj, "The purpose of the external guru is to help awaken the internal guru within each person. Therefore my work is to guide people in learning how to experience their own inner guide, to awaken them to an awareness of their own greater self. When this is accomplished, my guidance is no longer required, for each person becomes a guru unto himself."

Gururaj wanted people to know that he was just an ordinary human being, different from most individuals only in the fact that he had walked the spiritual path to the goal which the great majority of people are still striving to reach – enabling him to be useful as a guide. He repeatedly said that what he had attained, in his spiritual quest, all other human beings could also attain.

In accordance with this understanding, he insisted that he be treated as an ordinary human being with no more fuss or reverence than the dignity required by any person, and that IFSU in no way become a "cult of the guru". Gururaj's prime concern was to see IFSU become a worldwide fellowship of individuals on the path to fulfillment and self-realisation.

Meditation teaching groups affiliated to IFSU evolved in England, Ireland, Spain, USA, Canada, Denmark, Germany, Israel and South Africa. Several of these organisations hosted public talks, personal interviews, workshops and residential retreats centred on Gururaj who, during this period, spent more than half his life away from home advancing the spread of his teaching.

Gururaj was a key speaker and interviewee at the following:

World Parliament of Religions, Chicago, 1984 – The Wrekin Trust Symposium, "Mystics and Scientists," special guest of Sir GeorgeTrevelyn, King Alfred's College, England, 1979 – Holistic Health Symposium University of Nevada, Las Vegas, 1978 – International Neuropsychiatry Symposia, South Africa, 1982 – Annual Meeting of Association for Humanistic Psychology, Washington, D.C. 1982

Conferences/Retreats: Sociedad Española de Meditación – Dansk Meditation Samfund – British Meditation Society – American Meditation Society – Canadian Meditation Society – Irish meditation Society. *Newspapers/journals/TV*: Sunday Telegraph, London, April 1983 – Yoga Today, United Kingdom, 1984 (several articles) – Civilizations with Enrique Quesad, Madrid, Spain – Page 5 TV 5, Las Vegas, Nevada – Today in Chicago, CBS TV, Chicago – Focal Point, KTIV TV, Sioux City, IA – Party Line, NBC TV, Sioux Falls, S.D – Midday Am, NBC TV, St Louis – At Your Service, KMOX, CBS Radio, St Louis

Leaving his beloveds

Gururaj's health deteriorated from about 1984 onwards. Nevertheless he managed to get to residential retreats and tours, mainly in England, America, Canada and Spain throughout his final years. Sometimes he was so exhausted he would become unconscious for days on end. But he would not allow himself to be hospitalised. He would bounce back from each bout of illness like a spring lamb, to the amazement of everyone, declaring that he would serve mankind until his demise. Nevertheless his periods of good health became shorter. He died at his home in Cape Town on 17th May 1988 just days after returning from a tour of teaching on both sides of the Atlantic.

After Gururaj's passing a little disharmony set in for a while between some of his leading chelas because he had (apparently, it was revealed after his passing) made different statements to individuals close to him, which caused some conflict. Most chelas did not want one among them to become a family leader on the organisational front, because Gururaj had repeatedly said openly that every chela who had the determination to do so should do whatever he/she wished to do in order to promote the teachings to humankind.

The eventual outcome resolved the petty disagreements. Five new organisations – in England, Spain, Canada and Denmark – quickly got started to add to the seven already existing. Several more started in the following decade. More will undoubtedly develop. The strength of the bonds between Gururaj's chelas, established when he was alive, was sufficient to overcome the temporary differences and all the societies and groups – old and new – have established continued positive, productive, communication between them. This has helped expand the teaching throughout the world.

This all seems to be panning out in accordance with Gururaj's edicts that:

a) each should follow their own path; each person is individual and has their own view and their own skills in a work sense;

b) an individual in business on their own account is a supreme self-responsibility opportunity and benefit is gained from the growth opportunities;

c) an individual will put more effort into their own show than someone else's; and

d) one organisation growing too large is not good in respect of fairness because of the unnecessary power that inevitably ensues.

A great master has been in our presence. The love and spiritual energy radiating from this man, which was impossible to adequately describe during his life, is being transmitted to the world and is undoubtedly felt by those coming to his teaching – decades after his demise.

Lightning Source UK Ltd.
Milton Keynes UK

177910UK00001B/4/P